FAMILIES AROUND THE WORLD

FAMILIES AROUND THE WORLD

FAMILIES AROUND THE WORLD
© IMP AB 2007

CONTRIBUTORS

Text: Monica Berg, Magnus Falkehed, Gunilla Kinn, Kim Naylor, Lars Palmgren, Christer Petersson, Göran Svedberg, Nouha Taouk, Karin Tötterman, Martin Westholm

Pictures: Pierre Bassani, Jonas Gustavsson, Nikolaj and Katrin Jacobsen, Petter Johansson, Raul Lorca, Kim Naylor, Ivan Pavlovitj, Johan Pålsson, Páll Stefansson, Katarina Stoltz, Karin Tötterman

Graphic design: Petra Jisander Eriksson

Editor: Elisa Kvennborn

Translation: Samtext

EBS - Editoriale Bortolazzi Stei s.r.l.
Printed in Italy 2007

ISBN 10: 91-7002-514-2
ISBN 13: 978-91-7002-514-3

CONTENTS

FOREWORD

. . . .

It's exciting to see how other people design and furnish their homes! Gaining inspiration and learning something new; seeing things from a different perspective. What is an ordinary postcard rack for one person can be a rotating CD-storage unit for another. There are no rights and wrongs in interior design, so a couple of bass drums can become a sofa table. Let your imagination flow and find your own way. Perhaps this book can help you as you do so?

We've been invited to visit thirteen families from the four corners of the world. They've opened their homes to let us into their lives and their ideas on furnishings and the towns in which they live. Of course it's true that we're affected by where we live. Living in metro-politan Moscow is completely different from living in the sea port of Valparaiso. This is reflected in the way these homes are designed.

A home is a reflection of who we are and what we like. So it's exciting to visit these thirteen unique homes and share these families' realities and daily lives. Besides viewing each home, we'll also be invited to share exciting recipes and interesting facts about each country.

These families' doors are open, so open this book, enter their homes and be inspired!

Elisa Kvennborn

. . . .

BERLIN

Life and creativity in Mitte

LATITUDE 52° 31' N LONGITUDE 13° 25' E

FROM HIS DESK in the living room in old East Berlin, artist Holger Jacobs sees a world of creativity.

"This is the most creative place on the planet right now," he says, smiling dreamily.

He's visibly proud. Proud of his neighbourhood, his apartment and of being part of something bigger; right here and now.

In Berlin, Mitte district: latitude 52° 31' N, longitude 13° 25' E.

Here, where everything happens …

Below the window on just over seventy metres of pavement, a whole society comes together. There's a Muslim cultural association, a French bookshop, a feminist arts centre and a gay bar!

But there's no native Berliner in the building where Holger lives with his fifteen year-old son, Alexander. The neighbours come from either other European countries or from other towns in Germany.

"You see that singer there?" asks Holger pointing to his flat screen television screen in front of the living room sofa. On the screen, a little man is jumping onto a chair in front of a grand piano. You can feel the balmy background of a summer evening in a back yard. Holger's back yard.

"That singer, Thomas Quasthoff, has won four Grammys. He lives in this neighbourhood. It's a shame you didn't come last week, because he held a concert down here in the yard," says Holger as the amateur film rolls on. In his neigh-

bourhood, cultural life is on the boil. The neighbours arrange parties, concerts, exhibitions and boule tournaments.

Like Holger Jacobs, they're all hardened metropolitans.

For about ten years, Holger lived in Paris where he worked as a fashion photographer, commissioned by the most prestigious magazines: Harper's Bazaar, Vogue, L'Officiel …

"But I tired of that superficial world. I wanted to do something more stimulating and intellectual, to get involved with art," he says and shows his greatly enlarged art photographs that erase the borders between reality and dream, eroticism and fantasy …

A visit to a friend in East Berlin persuaded the newly divorced Holger Jacobs to take the leap.

"Dad asked me what I thought about moving to Berlin with him. It was a big change. A change in capital city, in life … An unbelievable challenge," says Alexander, now 15 years old.

He sits with his shoes pulled up onto the sofa that divides his room into two spacious halves. Like many Berliners, Holger wanted to send his son to an international school and Alexander found it quite easy to get into the highly acclaimed French school in Berlin, just a few underground stations away.

"When the wall came down, there were lots of French soldiers who moved home with their families," says Holger. Since then there've been lots of places for other pupils.

Together, Holger and Alexander moved into the light, three-roomed apartment on the second

THE APARTMENT
EXUDES MALE
HORMONES.

floor with a view over the Oranienburger square. The staircase on the way up smells of linoleum.

Inside the apartment, you're confronted with creaking pine floors and bright colours. Not aggressive, but a bit cheeky: turquoise with red, pink with white. On almost all of the walls, Holger has hung big pictures in the same shades of turquoise.

The three rooms are a mixture of apartment, exhibition hall and studio. In the combined studio and guest room stands a white tailor's dummy dressed in a tiny, red string thong. The apartment exudes male hormones.

The reason behind 50 year-old Holger's athletic physique hangs from the eleven-foot high ceiling in the form of a trapeze. In one corner, there is a pair of weights.

"I start each day with a little work-out," explains Holger.

Throughout his professional life, the former fashion photographer worked with beautiful bodies as a matter of course, so it's unthinkable that he would allow his own body to go downhill.

Holger is aware that he's cultivating a bit of a modern dandy image. At the end of the long corridor there are five different hats: a straw hat, a bowler hat, a felt hat …

"I bought this bowler hat when a theatre sold its store of props. I use it in the winter. The straw hat, which I wear during the summer months, is sold in a little shop in Mitte," explains Holger.

For him, it's important that the home functions, and not just as a home for him and Alexander. It's from here that the artist manages his

contacts with exhibitors and customers that are spread around the globe.

It's also here that he works and sometimes photographs. That's why the rooms are merged together.

The combined living room/bedroom/workroom and archive is dominated by a table in the centre. This is the connection point. A bookshelf with decades of photo archives cuts off part of the room and creates a wall between the TV corner and the archive. The archive shelves are hidden by a white curtain.

"The curtain prevents dust from getting onto the shelves," explains Holger.

For many people it would be difficult to separate the purposes for the different parts of the same surface. In many cases, dirty socks would have finished up on the worktable and work correspondence on the TV-sofa. A certain discipline is required for this kind of life.

But Holger doesn't see this as a problem.

"On the contrary! I appreciate everything being in its place."

On his three metre-long work table, he lays out the photographs that he's going to process. Five lamps, suspended at equal intervals and controlled by the same switch, provide perfect lighting for work.

Holger has a special working method for his pictures. First he takes photographs, then he scans his pictures, processes them in the computer and enlarges them. Finally, they become large frameless pictures. The work is time-consuming.

When hunger rears its head, the answer lies just below the window: the local kebab shop! There is no doubt in the Jacobs family that Berlin's kebabs are the best in Europe. They often solve the problem of dinner for Holger and Alexander. Neither of them is particularly keen on cooking. This also explains why the washing machine has taken over the dishwasher's central position in the kitchen.

The bright red refrigerator is mostly filled with breakfast food and some ready-made pasta sauces. In the beginning, Holger would have liked to see a refrigerator in pure 1950s style standing there. But instead it had to be an ordinary refrigerator, in bright red.

If you live in Mitte, you don't need to be a master chef. Just as the artists in Montmartre in Paris had access to some of the cheapest and most interesting restaurants, residents of Mitte have some of Berlin's best restaurants just round the corner. You only need to stroll down the street to find a genuine little restaurant where the wall seems to have preserved both decor and prices from before the Second World War.

The contrasts in this unique neighbourhood are stark. Totally dilapidated buildings support themselves against shining, newly-renovated facades. Many colourful back yards have been changed into galleries with outdoor cafes and shaded lawns.

"It's here that things are really happening. Everywhere, in every back yard and shop it's bubbling with life and creativity," says Holger.

Berliner Weiße mit Schuß
Green wheat beer

1 bottle of wheat beer (Weißbier)
1/2 schnapps glass of woodruff syrup

The picture shows the Berlin speciality Waldmeister grün, with sweet woodruff, but you can vary this with raspberry juice or other juices to taste. Drink with a thick straw!

He has his own explanation for it: Berlin is relatively cheap.

"Artists have always gravitated to towns where they can meet like-minded people and find large areas in which to live and work," he explains. On top of this, there's the logical effect of reunification:

"Since East and West came together, we have doubled the number of everything: theatres, opera houses and museums …"

Even today, there are dozens of properties with unknown owners. Many of these houses have been taken over by their occupants, some of whom have been living there for more than 15 years!

The fact is that it was the artists who were the first to stand up against the old communist regime. The former GDR government had far-reaching plans for demolishing the whole neigh-bourhood of Mitte with its worn turn-of-the Century architecture, stucco ceilings and winding staircases.

The artists protested and the plans never became reality.

On street corners, you can still come upon motorcycles and scooters from another era, an era when Lenin was a hero and a moped was treasured like the lifetime project that it actually was.

Even in Holger's home, there are traces of the Communist aesthetics of the artists' quarter. A kitschy television lamp with a shining waterfall is a reminder, like the cast iron mirror frame, of a time when aesthetics were part of a five-year plan.

"The television lamp provides a good light, so your eyes don't get tired in the darkness," says Holger and then picks up the little mirror:

"The factory that this mirror came from manufactured big iron pipes and gas pipes. But one day someone in the Politburo got the idea that people also needed a few beautiful things in their homes, so production was changed and this was the result. They're called consumer articles," explains Holger, holding up the mirror which has an ornate metal frame.

Holger likes the little mirror and the television lamp. They are testament to an era full of both shortages and hope. He refuses to set hard and fast limits between what is ugly or beautiful. It's about going on your feelings, in his opinion.

Like with the turquoise colour. It appeals to the artist in him, without him trying to understand why.

When he came across a large batch of turquoise curtains, he didn't hesitate for a second and bought more than all his windows would ever need. Then he

bought an equal number of red ones, plus a few pink curtains. Holger then hung the curtains on the walls of the studio/guest room.

"I'm free to remove them whenever I like. Or I can replace them with another colour according to my mood. Don't you agree, it's simpler than repainting the walls every time you want a new atmosphere in your room?"

Freedom is not an empty word in the Jacobs home. One of the reasons why Alexander is happy with his new life in Berlin.

"In Paris there was much that was so complicated: like meeting friends, and so on. Here everything is easier. I can go down to the cycle park with my friends or just nip over to their houses," says the fifteen year-old.

"In Paris it was usually the parents who planned their children's meetings. It felt a bit strange at times," Holger adds.

Alexander's freedom does have limits however. The television that used to stand in front of the sofa in his room has been replaced with a large, green pot-plant. And this isn't because Alexander loves horticulture.

"Not a lot of homework got done with the TV in the room," says Holger. Homework is the usual "excuse" for Alexander not having the time to shop or help with cooking.

"It's simple: Alexander does nothing in the kitchen!" says Holger with a tired smile.

But this won't prevent Alexander getting a brand new computer. At least as soon as father and son have ended their negotiations on how big the screen needs to be for Alexander to practice on his new drawing software.

"I'll also be getting a new desk. I've had this desk since I was little. Well, 10 years at any rate," says Alexander. The fifteen year-old's bed is already as big as his father's.

Generally, the two meet up in front of the television later in the evening. Unless Holger is relaxing in his Berlin bathroom.

Like most German bathrooms, it's spacious.

"You should be aware that it would have been even more spacious if the lift shaft hadn't taken up part of the room," Holger tells us.

The bathroom door has a small window covered over by a turquoise curtain.

When Holger moved in as the first tenant, he was allowed to influence the design of the bathroom. The result was a spacious jacuzzi with massaging water jets from all directions.

On the wall, he's rigged up stereo speakers and painted them in the same white colour as the tiles. The sound system's FM is tuned to one of Berlin's many jazz channels. Relaxation and harmony are important.

This is why Holger is a little curious about Chinese Feng Shui teaching and its advice on wind, water and interior design. In the guest room, which was originally intended to be Holger's own bedroom, the four-poster bed has been manufactured according to Feng Shui principles.

"I put those bamboo poles in the ceiling of the four-poster in a cross. It's more Feng Shui that way," says Holger.

But is it really a bed? Holger, who wanted a high bed, constructed a wooden cube. The ends were made from wooden slats, which are normally used in wooden decking in gardens.

"I thought it looked nice. I've also gained lots of storage space with this system," he explains proudly and lifts the mattress with its fake animal skin cover.

Storage space can be necessary in a room with no true corners for bookshelves. The studio/guest room is a typical *Berliner room*.

For some reason, Berlin's old buildings are full of strange rooms that seem to have been left over as dregs when the architects had finished the other parts of the apartments. They were left with odd angles and rooms that sometimes lacked windows.

In the Jacobs family's Berliner room, there's not only a window but also a small triangular balcony in the corner between two rooms. A few sunflowers are sweltering on the balcony. From there, you can see the back yard and cycle shed. Like any good Berliner, Holger has two bikes: one with heavier tyres for winter use and a lighter one for summer use. All he needs to discover a whole world.

BERLIN · GERMANY

Official name:
Bundesrepublik Deutschland/
Federal Republic of Germany

Official language: German

Capital city: Berlin

Area: 356,730 km²

Population: 82.5 million inhabitants

Population density:
231 inhabitants/km²

Currency: Euro, EUR

Internet users:
4,725 per 10,000 inhabitants

THE GOLDEN BEAR

The Berlin Film Festival, which enjoys great international prestige, was founded in 1951. The film awards consist of golden and silver bears given to filmmakers and actors from all over the world. Silver bears are awarded, amongst others, to Best Actor, Best Film Music and Best Director. Golden bears are awarded to the year's best film and as lifetime awards.

Films which have won the Golden Bear include: *Grbavica* (2006), *Spirited Away* (2002), *Sense and Sensibility* (1996), *She Danced One Summer* (1952).

THE OKTOBERFEST

At the end of September each year, one of Europe's biggest popular festivals begins: the Oktoberfest in Munich. During the festivities, around 7 million visitors consume 5 million litres of beer and over 200,000 sausages.

The Oktoberfest was originally celebrated to emphasise the end of one brewing season and the beginning of another. So the old beer had to be drunk before they could begin brewing the new.

BEER

Freising in Bavaria is the home of the world's oldest brewery, Weihenstephan's Brewery. Beer has been brewed here since the 11th Century.

The world's oldest food law also originated in Germany. This law stipulated that beer could only be brewed from hops, water, yeast and malt.

BAUHAUS

In Weimar in 1919, a school of art and crafts was founded under the name Bauhaus. This school has been one of the most influential in modern architecture and design.

The aim of the school was to do away with boundaries between arts and crafts and to integrate them in an architectural context.

Some Bauhaus products are still produced today, including the typical tubular steel furniture of Marcel Breuer and Ludwig Mies van der Rohe.

AUTOBAHN

The Autobahn, or German motorway network, consists of 10,900 km and is highly efficient. Along the Autobahn, there are 370 restaurants and no fewer than 354 petrol stations that are open 24/7.

The Autobahn is best known for having no speed limit. There is however a recommended top speed of 130 kmh, which is higher than in most countries.

LONDON

Modern living and a lot of nostalgia

JOELLE'S TEACAKE

200 g soft butter
200 g dark chocolate
4 eggs
200 g sugar
70 g flour

Heat oven to 180°C.
Melt butter and chocolate pieces.
Allow to cool.
Whisk together egg and sugar
in a bowl. Gradually whisk in the
butter and melted chocolate. Add
flour last. Mix well and pour into a
greased and floured cake tin. Bake
for 25–30 min. at 180°C.

SHOREDITCH IS NOT JUST ANY OLD PART of London. At first glance it's a rather run-down neighbourhood with workers' housing and shabby old industrial buildings.

But scratch the surface and you'll find something new, exciting and contemporary in this old industrial area of east London. The house we're visiting stands like a modern yellow and white lighthouse on a street where red double-decker buses roar past. Wood, brick and steel are used tastefully to frame the modern loft apartments.

Here in Shoreditch, the contrasts are abrupt and stark. Grubby workshops with car wrecks stand right next to chic houses with sports cars parked on the street. High-rises with nine floors

look down on cosy town-houses in the classical style.

We meet Joelle Talmasse as she storms into the little walkway that runs along the facade and outside the front doors of the second floor. She smiles apologetically whilst she rummages frantically for her keys in her large shoulder-bag.

"The traffic was terrible! I had to visit a customer after dropping off the children at playschool," she explains one cup of tea later as she begins to relax.

We're sitting at a round, green metal table in the middle of a light and airy room. The lively London traffic is reduced to a barely audible buzz. Her teacake leaves large, inviting crumbs on the table.

This is how Joelle wants her life: Stress and frenzy outside, tea and cake in the peace of her home.

She is an interior designer and thinks that homes, her own as well as others, are the most exciting things of all. It's been like that since her childhood.

"I grew up with this interest. My mother lived with a noted furniture collector. Furniture has always been something special for me."

Joelle is constantly on the hunt for furniture: In antique shops, at flea markets …

"… and sometimes even in rubbish containers! That postcard rack which is now a CD-rack is a rubbish container find," she says, smiling at the memory of this discovery.

"I found it after the removal lorry had driven away from my former home. They had to turn back and take it with them as well."

Joelle's latest drug, as she describes it, is Internet auctions.

Now, at the age of 39, it's the 1970s of her childhood that she loves to revisit and put into new contexts. Not to create a museum or a vintage collection of objects from a bygone era:

"I think that people often collect 1970s objects in a silly and thoughtless way."

Joelle likes to mix 1970s objects with ethnic styles. She even does it in the way she dresses. Today she's wearing a striped 70s shirt with a Mao collar and a necklace from West Africa.

In order to better demonstrate what she means, we climb up the little staircase to the loft. On an angular sofa lies an African plaid, a small wooden box stands out against a desktop with typical 1975 geometry. She's resolutely covered the desktop with ordinary wallpaper in a red-brown-black pattern that she liked!

"I think the ethnic style fits in well, it softens the often strict and angular pattern that you find in this type of furniture. I also happen to work with a couple of South Africans in a design company," she says.

The treasure that Joelle is really proud of is a little desk that stands next to the bed. A design enthusiast would notice that it's a genuine Giancarlo Piretti creation from 1969. Joelle also sees something else in it: her childhood!

"I had a table exactly like that in my room when I was little. I spent many long hours at that table. You can guess how happy I was when I found the *Plia* chair from the same collection in a little shop," she says, smiling dreamily.

Above the table is a storage unit made of plastic. It's Dorothée Maurer's legendary *Ustensilo* from 1970. But instead of pens and paperclips, Joelle adorns it with flowers and small postcards.

Rummaging through shops and flea markets is Joelle's biggest pastime. No surprise then that it was on the famous market Street, Portobello Road, that she met her husband Massimo Bertoni.

They both lived in Notting Hill at the time.

"But then the film *Notting Hill* came out with a whole circus in its wake. Today Notting Hill is a haven for bankers and Porsches. It's all just got too much, quite simply," says Massimo when he arrives home from work.

He's not a banker himself, but a Fleet Street stockbroker. Living in an area of town where all his colleagues were moving in was unthinkable for him:

"I like swimming against the stream, not following everyone else all the time."

When Notting Hill changed into a film set, the couple decided to move east instead, to Shoreditch. It's one of the last areas of London where you can still see large workshop premises and deserted factories.

Or as the taxi driver explained on the way here:

"Here, everything can change from one street to the next; not to mention from one side of the street to the other. Look over there, on the left: shabby local authority housing and there, on the right, a chic newly built house!"

From one of the shabbier buildings opposite Joelle and Massimo's house rises an enormous red brick factory chimney. Today it's a theatre.

If you turn your back to the theatre you see the "Gherkin", a well-known silhouette from the wealthy City.

If, on the other hand, you walk outside the apartment door, from the walkway you will see long rows of glazed industrial buildings from the turn of the last century.

Today, many of these have been taken over by people from creative professions such as artists, advertising people and fashion designers.

The fashion designer Alexander McQueen was first to arrive a few years ago. Today, a stream of different trendsetters is moving towards East London.

In nearby Hoxton Square, world famous artists such as Gilbert and George or Sophie Calle exhibit. Building cranes rise up in every direction. While Turkish and Indian merchants get on with their lives amid a welter of spicy aromas.

For the new professional groups needing large areas in which to exhibit, it's not easy to keep up with the price rises in London's housing market. Nor is it easy for anyone else for that matter:

"It's gone completely mad," says Massimo.

"Today you can't talk to a Londoner for more than two minutes before the housing situation comes up in the conversation: who lives where and what it costs," he says.

The fact that every square metre is worth its weight in gold has resulted in a phenomenal interest in renovation.

"I'm more of a cat myself. I've got about the same tastes as Joelle, when it comes to interiors. But it bothers me when Joelle comes home dragging the fifty-ninth vase or table. I like my existence to be pretty stable, but generally still appreciate a change after a while. When I've got used to the novelty," says Massimo.

"I must admit that I sometimes have a tendency to buy more tables than there are chairs for and more vases than there are tables to put them on," says Joelle.

If there's enthusiasm for interior design in Massimo and Joelle's home, there's complete renovation-hysteria in the rest of London:

"People would rather spend money on paint and wallpaper than clothes, for example," says Massimo and uncorks a bottle of wine.

The fact that Joelle and Massimo have an open-plan living room and kitchen is not by chance. Space is money …

Massimo is not always satisfied with what he sees around him. Not even in his own building. It's the standardisation that disturbs the individualist in him, the fact that seventy apartments in his building can have the same wooden floors and the same kitchens. Not that they're ugly, but conformism disturbs him:

"Usually I don't like things to be vulgar or common."

The apartment building in which Joelle and Massimo live is of the ultra-modern variety. Even the electrical sockets are exquisite in their luxurious chrome fittings. The facade is a mixture of concrete and wooden slats. It filters the daylight pleasantly in front of enormous windows.

On the balcony outside their loft, Massimo loves to sit and relax with a newspaper or a book on sunny days.

In reality, he views himself as an aesthete. An aesthete who fell in love with an artist. One day

he'll take up art photography as a hobby again; he's promised himself. Art photography has taken a back seat in the past few years for the benefit of children and work.

"I like things to be in harmony. Like the colours in that painting: they contrast with the drawing that my daughter did today," he says, pointing to the desk against the wall where the drawing is placed under the painting in question.

The painting he points to was done by Joelle, who is an artist as well as an interior designer. She paints in large, sweeping strokes of colour pigment and glue.

"I like that enlarged feeling which is brought out. When you enlarge a picture till it becomes unclear, it's the pigment that remains together with a 'dusty' impression," she says when she shows the other painting on the loft staircase. It's situated in one of the few places in the apartment not literally bathed in light. Joelle's art is often inspired by oriental kelim carpets like the one on the wood floor in the combined living room and kitchen:

"I've always been fascinated by kelim carpets. Did you know that the women who weave them also weave in small hidden messages into the carpets? They're often about hopes for good fortune and love …"

You won't find dust anywhere other than on the art in Joelle's home. In spite of the two small girls who like to tumble around here: Amalia and Olivia. Their room is under the loft, to the left of the entrance.

When the girls started to crawl and walk, many of Joelle's friends advised her to put away all the beautiful vases and other things. But the mother-of-two refused to do this:

"I don't think it's wrong for children to learn to respect certain things in a home," she explains. Despite the fact that Amalia and Olivia love to

romp around on the stairs and sofas, the ornaments are still intact.

One of the kids' favourite places seems to be the pistachio-green vintage sofa with its matching and equally pistachio-green table lamp. But neither parent appears to be worried by the children playing among these treasures.

Joelle thinks the idea that children are incompatible with city life is nonsense. At least if the city is London. It's energising to listen to everything that Joelle has to say about parents and children in London. After a while, it's almost hard to understand how a family with children can actually live *anywhere else* than in this pulsating metropolis!

"The local authority does everything it can to stop mothers from being isolated. There are crèches and mothers' groups and playgroups. You can have your children looked after while you talk to other parents. This is because of the fear that lone parents can suffer from depression and lots of other things," she tells us.

Joelle's and Massimo's girls go to a pony club; they swim and play at kindergarten. The kindergarten is right next door to a pre-school for autistic children. Everything is done so that children with different backgrounds and abilities will get to know each other. And become true Londoners one day.

"And on top of this there are all the free museums and all the other activities for children," says Joelle.

Both girls love picture books. But one of Olivia and Amalia's favourite

activities is being eaten up. Eaten up by a long and not very frightening monster in the park below their building:

"It's a snake! It eats children!" Olivia tells us.

The long climbing frame with built-in slide dominates the park next to Hagerston Road. The girls also love buying flowers with their mother. They are allowed to choose the colours and varieties for themselves. Their favourite place for buying flowers is Columbia Flower Market.

As we're going to a little art gallery in this neighbourhood, Joelle pulls out her car keys.

"It's a bit of a walk otherwise," she says apologetically, and we soon realise that she was right. What looks like a five-minute walk on a map of London often takes more than half an hour once you've started walking.

"This town is so unbelievably spread out. And the traffic is a disaster. Between fetching the children and visiting customers I probably spend around twenty-five hours a week in my car," says Joelle.

London's outer ring-road, the M25, is 190 km long! It's longer than a return journey to the coastal resort of Brighton from central London. Seen from space, the capital looks like a large twinkling star on the English countryside.

"I do the work of thinking and drawing during the evenings and nights," she says. One of her clients is a chic furniture shop on the Portobello Road. As well as selling furniture, they also manage design projects. Here Amalia and Olivia run between Chinese lamps and Vietnamese lacquer cupboards as if they'd been doing it all their lives.

Massimo often works late too, both in and out of the office.

"In my job, customer contacts are important. In the City, it's important to know what's going on at all times. A lot of time is spent socialising with clients, even in the evenings."

When the couple occasionally has the time to visit a restaurant together, it's often a little Indian hole-in-the-wall restaurant, in Brick Lane for example. The lively market street is full of small, inexpensive restaurants.

"Here you can buy the best salt beef bagels in London! It's completely unpretentious and I don't know what they do with the meat, but it's unbelievably delicious!" says Massimo.

If they'd prefer to eat at a gastro-pub with a trendy menu, then that's no problem either. Which Massimo and Joelle seem to find unfortunate, given that waistlines tend to expand rather than shrink.

"Today it seems as though all London pubs are being converted into gastro-pubs! Try finding a pub that serves ordinary decent fish and chips – it's almost impossible!" they say in unison.

They have an explanation for the gastronomic revolution that has swept the country. Britain used to be notorious for its awful food.

"But then the Brits started to travel around the world and asked the question: Why should I put up with food like this when everyone else in the world is eating better?" Joelle explains.

When Massimo and Joelle stay at home in the kitchen, there could be chicken or lamb on the menu, or why not fish or shellfish? And often with exotic spices.

"I love to experiment with chicken in lots of different ways. For example with lemon and various spices stuffed under the skin of the chicken," says Joelle.

Afterwards they like to watch DVDs up in the loft. "DVDs – not television," Massimo tells us:

"It's quite nice, actually. The only thing I miss sometimes is the news. But I can get it on the Internet or from newspapers," he says. It is important that nothing disturbs the peace and quiet of the home.

LONDON · GREAT BRITAIN

Official name: United Kingdom of Great Britain and Northern Ireland

Official language: English

Capital city: London

Area: 244,230 km²

Population: 59.3 million inhabitants

Population density:
243 inhabitants/km²

Currency: British pound, GBP

Internet users:
4,231 per 10,000 inhabitants

TAXIS

London has the world's best taxi service. You just need to take one of the black taxi cabs. In order to become a black taxi driver, you have to pass difficult tests to prove your knowledge of London. It takes time to be approved. It can take up to four years before you get the much longed-for badge. Besides knowledge of London and its road network, the character of prospective cabbies is tested and a check is carried out in the crime register.

BIG BEN

It isn't the tower that is called Big Ben, but the actual bell. The clock tower is called Saint Stephen's Tower.

PADDINGTON STATION

The beloved bear Paddington was named after the underground station at Paddington Station in London.

Paddington's "daddy" is Michael Bond who bought the bear as a present for his wife for Christmas 1956. The first book about Paddington came out in 1958.

AFTERNOON TEA

Anna, the 7th Duchess of Bedford, was the person who introduced *afternoon tea* in the 1700s. She discovered that if you drink tea at four or five o'clock in the afternoon, this can reduce the hunger pangs that can come between lunch and dinner.

Another person who influenced English habits at social gatherings was the Earl of Sandwich. He came up with the idea of putting a filling between two slices of bread – and the sandwich was born.

The Brits drink 165 million cups of tea a day.

BLOODY MARY

The drink Bloody Mary has a bloody history. It was named after the English queen, Mary I, who lived 1516–58.

Mary was a devout Catholic who reintroduced Catholicism to England through a bloody massacre of 300 heretics. This got her the nickname of Bloody Mary, now also the name of the famous vodka and tomato juice drink with Tabasco, pepper and celery.

STOCKHOLM

Double living. Double happiness.

STOCKHOLM IS BUILT ON islands, islets and skerries. The Stockholm archipelago contains no less than 24,000 islands, of which 150 are inhabited throughout the year.

The inner city, the part of Stockholm that is situated within the old marine Customs area, consists of fourteen larger islands. And when Stockholm grows, it spreads out sideways. It grows inland and outwards to the islands in the sea.

Eva and Valle have just moved to Hammarby Sjöstad, one of Stockholm's newest residential areas, just south of the inner city. The sea is just a stone's throw from the thirty square metre patio and there's a slalom slope just behind the houses.

"In the wintertime, it is possible to ski down from the top of the slope to the local pub, Göte-borg, where we can partake of après-ski. We can then take the boat which is only a few metres from the pub and continue the evening at Stureplan.

"And with the shuttle-train, bus or boat, it takes only fifteen minutes to get to the centre of Stockholm.

We love Hammarby Sjöstad," Eva tells us. "It's so beautiful with all the water, the wide boulevards, pleasant local pubs and a living town centre. Despite the fact that it's a newly built part of town, there's an inner-city feeling about it."

Both Eva and Valle are fairly typical modern Stockholmers in the middle of their lives and careers. They met eleven years ago and moved

together into Eva's little two room apartment on Kungsholm in central Stockholm where they lived together with their son, Philip.

"We belong to the generation of Stockholmers for whom housing is not something that you get automatically," Eva informs us. Tenancies inside the Customs area are very rare and the housing association properties are terribly expensive.

"Right up until the spring, after twenty years of waiting, when the housing authority offered us this fantastic 120 m² in Hammarby Sjöstad, we'd been living in cramped two-roomed apartments with no room for us or the furniture."

For Eva, Valle and Philip, more spacious accommodation in one of the sleepy villa suburbs has never been an option. Eva works as a freelance fashion stylist, running between newspapers, fashion shows and shops day and night.

"My job isn't just a job," she explains. "It's a lifestyle. I live and work in the heart of the city. I neither can nor will settle down on a suburban sofa and fall asleep in front of the telly.

"I work very hard." A normal working day for Eva usually doesn't end before midnight.

For his part, Valle works as a house designer for a land and property company. He was once a carpenter, but took a course in computing almost ten years ago.

"The body just breaks down with the pace on modern building sites. I wanted to quit before I finished up in pain all over."

Philip has just finished at secondary school and intends continuing to university. But like more and more young people in Sweden, he's chosen to live at home while he studies in order not to incur too much debt. It's also difficult to find cheap student flats in Stockholm. And charming little one-roomed apartments with low rents are a thing of the past.

Tor, Philip's half-brother, also lives with Eva and Valle during weekends, summer holidays and at other times.

Thus, the Lindh-Wallström family are typical Stockholmers. They have a large group of half-siblings, step-parents and biological ties, plus a dog called Charlie.

Never before has Stockholm had such a large dog population. In the dog-walking areas of the city's parks it's easy to see what the city's favourite breeds are: Danish-Swedish farm dogs (like Charlie), Rhodesian Ridgebacks and the Lagotto, an Italian truffle hound.

Stockholm has many dog day-centres, but since he was a puppy, Charlie has been used to going with Eva on her rounds of editorial meetings and fashion shows:

"Dogs of this breed aren't suited to staying at home alone, they just cry all the time!" But Charlie's small and easy to handle, so it's no problem having him with her.

In a two-roomed apartment it finally became too cramped for all of them. As mentioned previously, a more spacious home in the suburbs was out of the question.

GRILLED PERCH

4 portions

4 perch, approx. 1½ kg

1½ tsp salt

2 table spoons of oil

50–75 ml mayonnaise

100 ml sour cream

50 ml whipping cream

1–2 tsp freshly squeezed
   lemon juice

salt, freshly ground white or
   black pepper

Scale the perch under cold water. Rinse the fish, clean them and cut off the heads.

Make some cuts into the back of the perch and rub in salt.

Mix the mayonnaise and sour cream. Whip the cream and mix it with the lemon juice and mayonnaise mixture. Season with salt and pepper. Pour the sauce into a serving dish. Place in refrigerator for 15 min.

Brush the perch with oil. Place on a grill or gridiron so that they can be easily turned. Grill for 5 min. on each side.

Serve immediately with lemon sauce, boiled or mashed potatoes and leeks fried in butter.

"That's why we decided to buy a spacious summer house," Valle explains.

A quiet oasis, far from the tarmac and traffic, but near enough to commute to the town's offices, editors and watering holes.

A house and some land with space, light and silence.

A place where they could determine everything; every little nook and cranny and every doorhandle and where there was a place for all the stored furniture from the cellar.

A life project and pension plan all in one.

It's one of life's ironies that in the very year the summer house was finally ready, the apartment in Hammarby Sjöstad came up. Now they have plenty of space. All the year round.

In a sheltered bay in the middle of the Stockholm archipelago on Timrarö island, forty kilometres from the city, stands Eva and Valle's white summer house. It was inspired by late 19th Century architecture; like a miniature wholesaler's villa.

"The location is perfect!" says Valle. The office in town is only 40 minutes away, door-to-door.

With a laptop and mobile Internet connection, the distance shrinks yet further. Working hours are no longer so tied to the office.

The bay, known as Grandmother's Bay, is silent. The winds are seldom strong here.

Even when the big passenger ferries sail past the island on their way to Finland, it isn't that noticeable.

It was in Grandmother's Bay that the island's first house was built in the 17th Century. Today there are around forty houses spread around the island, of which eight are new buildings. But there's nothing else there. No shops, no cars, no services. Valle installed the water supply himself.

"We have a close, warm relationship with the other new home owners on the island because we all help each other out when problems arise. We've made lots of new friends on this tiny little island."

During the summer before they began to build the house, Eva and Valle were often out on the island to see how the light behaved. All of the rooms and windows in the house are designed according to the way the sun moves over the plot.

"Natural light is the light source that we live and work by."

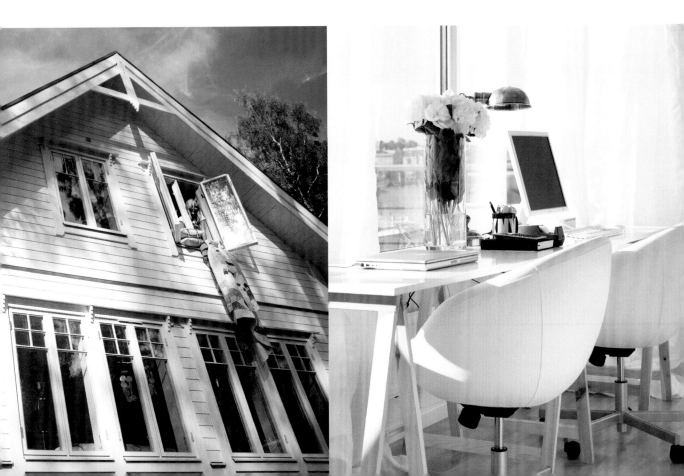

LIGHT IS
          IMPORTANT,
     AS ARE
DETAILS.

The hill behind the house provides shade and darkness in the bedroom, whilst the daylight illuminates via the glossy white wooden floors in the kitchen. The evening sun shines on the glass veranda of the upper floor.

But, despite all the drawings and calculations, things never work out exactly as planned.

"We wanted to build a year-round dwelling, so that we can gradually move back to the island when we retire. But it was too expensive. If you build on an island, you have to reckon on everything costing around 40 percent more."

On the other hand, it emerged that the bedrock was lower than expected.

"So we got a 70 m² cellar – completely unexpectedly!"

Light is important, as are details. Eva and Valle were both agreed that they didn't want any standard solutions for the cupboards, bathroom, doors, etc.

So they've changed and improved all visible details to a more personal style; standard doors in natural wood, for example, were given an old charm by white glazing and new locks in a Turn-of-the-Century style.

"We've had to compromise," says Eva. "For Valle, high-tech is important. We have some ultramodern elements, such as an elegant espresso machine, a high-tech hob with plate-warmer and so on. Whilst I've been able to wallow in flowers and delicate lace."

Eva loves beautiful things. She's been collecting furniture, fabrics and other things from all over the world for twenty years. Things she didn't know what to do with, until now.

In the bathroom there's a beautiful hand basin that she bought from a hotel in Hua Hin in Thailand. On one of the short walls of the upper floor hang two beautiful oars, rescued from a bonfire and hung up as ornaments.

All the beds are generously made up with striped, chequered and floral textiles, and on top are genuine old patchwork quilts from markets that Eva visited in Los Angeles twenty years ago.

An old clothes cupboard is the only clothes storage unit in the house.

"Wardrobes just collect things that people never use," explains Eva. "Out here, we don't need

anything that we can't keep in the clothes cupboard."

She has however bought an ordinary steel clothes rail that she's glazed in white. On it hangs a row of beautiful, delicate dresses in the bedroom.

"Sometimes I buy clothes just because they're beautiful. They look good as a still life."

For a fashion shoot, Eva also made up an arrangement of old lace collars which she hung in the beautiful Italian silk lamp above the dining room table.

"I think it's nice that they can hang there."

The living room's round, open fireplace is surrounded by hand-picked stones from the south coast's shores. Farthest away in one corner of the room is a large old birdcage that has finally found

its place. Beside the birdcage is a worn dining table from Denmark which now serves as a bookshelf.

"The books and magazines are more accessible if they're served up on a table, just as the toilet rolls in the bathroom are if they're placed in a beautiful old vase, and the shower towels when they're hung on a bamboo ladder."

Swedish interest in plants and gardens has blossomed in recent years, perhaps as a natural accompaniment to the huge interest in interior design.

The latest trend is natural gardens with flowers in pots on stone-paved terraces and greenhouses with vines, citrus trees and vegetables.

Eva and Valle have planned their garden in this way. In front of the door stand pink hydrangeas, planted in stainless steel buckets.

"Hydrangeas are one of the few flowers that I think are beautiful even when they've dried," Eva tells us.

In the ditches, they have planted clover and meadow flowers and beyond the lawn are 14 newly-planted Himalayan birches with extra-white trunks. They are struggling to get the newly-sown grass to grow as high and wild as possible and in one corner there is an English-style greenhouse.

There is an extra room, instead of a terrace and veranda. Somewhere to sit when it's raining or when the north wind is blowing.

"But I've left room in two corners to plant grapevines. They are decorative and prevent people looking in. There's also room for tomato plants."

The next project is to build a bathhouse down by the jetty. "In the countryside, you need a place where you can rinse off dirty boots, wash the dog – and scrub yourself clean from head to toe."

Eva is an enthusiastic winter bather.

"Plunging into a hole in the ice after heating up your body in a sauna is better than any spa in the world," she says enthusiastically. "It gives you such a kick!"

In the bathhouse there will be a wood-fired sauna and a wooden barrel full of cold water to sink down into afterwards.

It's the simplicity of living close to nature that's so nice. Collecting rainwater in a wine barrel outside the door. Picking your food directly from the garden.

Eva does use the summerhouse as a studio for fashion photography, but above all it gives her and Valle inspiration. Peace and quiet.

"When we're out here we never watch television," says Valle. "We disconnect from all media. Here, we're so far away from everything."

And yet so close.

STOCKHOLM • SWEDEN

Official name: Konungariket
Sverige/The Kingdom of Sweden

Official language: Swedish

Capital city: Stockholm

Area: 410,934 km^2

Population: 9.01 million inhabitants

Population density:
22 inhabitants/km^2

Currency: Swedish krona, SEK

Internet users:
5,731 per 10,000 inhabitants

SINGING AT SKANSEN

A summer event that is close to the
hearts of Swedes is the television
programme *Singing at Skansen*. The
programme has been recorded since
1979 in the open air museum
Skansen at Djurgården in Stockholm.

The programme includes both
Swedish and international artistes.
The high point of the programme is
the communal singing, when the
artiste chooses a song that he/she
performs together with the audience.

The programme has very high

viewing figures, but it's also popular
to be part of the audience. People
start queuing outside Skansen early
in the morning (03:00) in order to get
good seats!

MIDSUMMER

Celebrating Midsummer is an old
Swedish tradition. Originally, the
summer solstice was celebrated, i.e.
the longest day and shortest night. It
was a night filled with magic and
superstition.

When Sweden became Christian-
ised, the birth of John the Baptist was
integrated into the celebrations. Despite the Christian element, Midsummer Night has retained its magic and
much of the old superstition lives on
today, including the custom of collecting seven sorts of flowers and laying
them under your pillow on midsummer
night in order to dream about your
future husband or wife.

ASTRID LINDGREN

One of the world's foremost children's
authors is Astrid Lindgren (1907–
2002).

Astrid Lindgren's books have been
translated into 76 languages and have
sold over 80 million copies the world
over. Her most popular children's
character is Pippi Longstocking; the
books about Pippi have been translated into 51 different languages.

EVERYMAN'S RIGHT

Swedes have always had a close and
fond relationship with nature, mani-

fested in a unique law called Everyman's Right.

Everyman's Right means that everyone has the right to spend time in
the countryside provided that he or
she does not disturb nature and animal life. It is permissible to pick all
berries, fungi and flowers that are not
officially protected.

As you are allowed to go onto
private land in the countryside, it is
important to show the landowners
respect and not go too near their
homes or destroy property.

PARIS

We live in a shop window!

THEIR LIFE IS A SHOW. The Parisians, Erwin and Jean-Christophe transformed their home into a luxurious showroom and a three-star B&B – without being rich themselves!

Today they live like goldfish in a diamond-studded crystal bowl.

On the door of their castle-like house of brick, there are three doorbells to choose from. After three rings on as many buttons, footsteps can be heard.

"*Bonjour!* Come in!" says Jean-Christophe Stoerke, as he opens the solid oak door. He is dressed in faded jeans and a T-shirt. To the right of the entrance hall, a narrow staircase leads both up and down. Which explains the three doorbells.

"Coffee?"

The answer leads us down to a state-of-the-art kitchen in brilliant white with clean work surfaces in some kind of concrete.

"It's called Stac. It was invented by a chemist in Marseille," explains Jean-Christophe. The design is signed Damien Langlois-Meurinne.

But what really bewitches the visitor is the view from the window: the fairytale garden!

Jean-Christophe has created every Parisian landscape designer's dream – a large town garden with the Eiffel Tower as decor!

In Jean-Christophe's garden, there is also a shining white baldachin bed, squeezed in between the bamboo and the straight lines of flowers.

Lying down on this bed, you get a complete view of the house which extends over six floors.

"Seven if you count a little wine cellar," Jean-Christophe corrects us.

A little while later he produces his mobile phone and rings the fifth floor:

"Erwin, could you bring me down a clean shirt when you come, please?"

Jean-Christophe lives here together with the actor and playwright Erwin Zirmi.

Their home is a project: A business project, an art project and a life project!

We walk up the garden steps to the living room. Everything there is of the finest quality, from curtains to sofas and parasols. The small black coffee tables appear, like everything else, to come from expensive design manufacturers. Which they do.

The mosquito-net-like curtains on the veranda windows come from one of the world's most exclusive textile designers. When the curtains slide over each other they create a dancing and shimmering moiré effect in the light.

There's just one tiny drawback:

"None of this belongs to us," says Erwin with a sweeping gesture.

"We haven't got any real savings. We live well, but like millions of other people we have to watch every penny," says Jean-Christophe in his newly ironed shirt.

"If you look more closely, for example at the parasol, you can see that there's a label on it with the name of the manufacturer." The manufacturers that Jean-Christophe uses in his work have

been persuaded to exhibit their products free in the landscape and interior designer's home:

"My customers, like many others who come here, can see their products in a completely different environment. But the most important thing is that this is a decor that I can take charge of."

Even so, friends wonder if the arrangement doesn't feel like living in a shop window: Jean-Christophe is 36, Erwin is 31. They belong to the Big Brother-generation. Is this the ultimate consequence of docusoaps? Modern living: a sponsored life for hire, continuously judged by friends and acquaintances. The living room with its large verandas onto the boulevard has the attributes of an aquarium, with us as the goldfish!

"I don't care. As far as I'm concerned, I could settle down anywhere. I'm not as attached to things as Jean-Christophe," Erwin explains leaning back on a luxurious garden sofa with geometrical, grey cushions next to the mantelpiece. On the wall behind him is an enormous plasma screen.

"But we really are living a little like the Frenchmen who came back from Algeria when it became independent: empty-handed!" he smiles.

Erwin is actually a finance and tax expert, but he never pursued that career. Instead he was an actor in one of France's docusoaps, *Le Pensionnat de Chavagnes*. He played a strict history teacher in a boarding school. Today he's working on writing and producing a comedy for one of Paris's privately-owned theatres. It's about a woman who's approaching 40 and wants a child at any price.

Everything in this house has been thought through. In front of the hearth is a fireguard of pure glass with neither frame nor decoration. Pure minimalism, like the flat curve of the wood basket.

Instead of a ceiling, the architect has created a big opening between the two floors. A long, dark piece of textile with laser-perforated flower pattern hangs down the greyish-white wall along the two levels.

On the mantelpiece stands a small baroque statuette with cherubs at play as counterpoint to the other straight lines and surfaces.

"This is Jean-Christophe's gift. He has the ability to emphasise things that, seen on their own, could be seen as ugly. But he can make them beautiful by placing them in the right context. Like those two Swedish cushions with the floral embroidery. When he came home with these, I wondered what on earth he would be able to do with them. But on that sofa they look perfect," says Erwin, pointing to the cushions.

And it's the same with the blue and orange shower cubicle standing at the entrance to the garden. However fabulous the catalogue or showroom it was displayed in, it would still just look like a chic shower cubicle for the beach. No more, no less.

But in Jean-Christophe and Erwin's home it resembles a stylish sentry box ... despite the fact that it's used to store rubbish! Inside the sentry box is the house wheelie-bin in regulation green, just like every other wheelie-bin in Paris! This is an idea that many customers would probably never have thought of if they hadn't seen it here. The difference with a showroom is that here the rubbish is real:

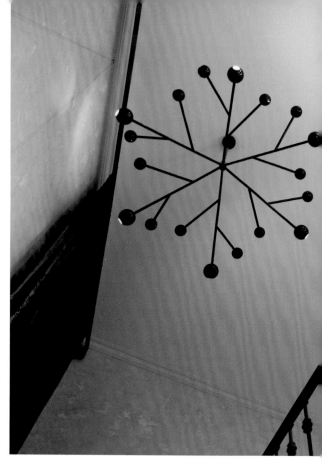

"I have to roll it out onto the pavement every morning before seven when the rubbish collection vehicle comes. If you put it out later, you get fined," Jean-Christophe explains.

We climb the narrow wood-panelled staircase. It creaks a little underfoot. Jean-Christophe tells us that the house was built in 1883 – the epoch when Oscar Wilde fled from British puritanism and ultimately ended his days in Paris.

The house's first owner was an art-lover who lived here with his servant, who was actually his boyfriend. When the owner died, he left the house to his boyfriend/servant.

"I think it's a beautiful story," says Jean-Christophe. He and Erwin are renting the house. This is the third home that they've shared. First they lived in a one-roomed apartment of 35 m² with a sleeping alcove. Then they moved to a

AREN'T THEY TOO LONG?
– *Oh non!* THAT'S WHAT
MAKES THEM SO CHIC!

two-roomed apartment of 50 m² with a dining table in the entrance hall. Today they have 180 m² of living space over six floors!

"The house is very French! That means that the architect put the emphasis on charm rather than practicality," Jean-Christophe explains.

We come up to the drawing room. From a loft-like balcony we look down on the suite of furniture around the fireplace. The same perforated textiles hang on the walls.

A white coffee table stands out against the prevailing beige and black tones of the room. The table is reminscent of the 1970s design in the film *A Clockwork Orange* and its Korova Milkbar. The wood floor has a light, slightly Scandinavian patina. The windows are hung with beige and brown chiffon curtains in a classical cut. The curtains hang onto the floor. But aren't they too long?

"*Oh non!* That's what makes them so chic! Having curtains that reach just to the floor would be cheap. Like wearing trousers that are too short, showing your socks underneath," says Jean-Christophe, looking down at his own frayed jeans which drag a little under his soles.

If there's one thing that he and Erwin can't stand, it's cheating. Things that pretend to be what they're not.

"It's like things that have been made too quickly or carelessly. I find that unbelievably irritating. Not to mention when people try to hide manufacturing faults. That sort of thing can drive me crazy," Jean-Christophe says vehemently.

He proudly repeats a comment that an extremely elegant lady made about this room:

– "Darling it's so diva!" Jean-Christophe imitates an upper class French accent. But the most diva-esque thing of all is best seen from the balcony and runs along the whole facade on this floor.

From the balcony there's a wonderful view of the Eiffel Tower, seen between the leaves of the maple trees. Every evening after sunset, the tower sparkles and glitters. Later, the tower turns into a gigantic lighthouse with beams of light sweeping across the whole of the French capital.

"That was a fantastic idea that they came up with for the millennium," says Jean-Christophe and continues:

"That tower never ceases to fascinate me. Every time I see it, I stop for a minute and look at it!"

Along the balcony rail hang flower baskets. In them, Jean-Christophe has planted splendid green plants with huge leaves. Opposite the house, on the other side of the boulevard, is a churchyard. A stone's throw to the left is the Place Trocadéro. Pure film set, in other words.

"I feel a bit like Marie-Antoinette in Sophia Coppola's film. She lived in the middle of that royal court without really belonging to it," says Erwin.

He describes the neighbourhood as a microcosm for the upper class. But at the same time Erwin loves this Paris; strolling on the boulevards, visiting the luxurious cafés and rummaging through books and CDs in the department stores.

All of that superficial have-you-seen-me-and-who-are-you?-Paris, that sometimes disturbs Jean-Christophe, doesn't bother Erwin in the slightest.

Jean-Christophe also comes from the provinces. More precisely from Nancy, which is on the border with Germany.

"It's a town with strong artistic and industrial roots," says Jean-Christophe. He would like to move to the countryside one day. He's long dreamt of a charming B&B in the French countryside. This dream has now been fulfilled, except for one detail: his B&B is in Paris!

Jean-Christophe and Erwin have had one of the rooms in the house converted to a luxury bed and breakfast suite.

"I'm really a country boy. But Erwin was upset about my dream of a country B&B. This solution is a compromise," says Jean-Christophe.

The guest room is also furnished with exclusive textiles and designer lamps. One difference

"It's simple: I love this city! I'm a highly militant Paris-lover. It's not only the world's most beautiful city. It's the world's most practical city to live and move around in. I mean, Venice and London might be beautiful, but they're hardly practical," says Erwin.

Like most Parisians, Erwin comes from the provinces.

Erwin Zirmi's family tree is like a textbook of modern French history. His grandfather, who was a Berber, moved from North Africa to Brittany in western France.

"There he learned Breton in the belief that it was French," Erwin tells us. Later he moved inland and ran a small, local empire of hairdressing salons in Amiens. In northern France.

ma racine est au fond des bois, au bord des s

perhaps is that the colours are warmer and cosier here, like the chiffon curtains in plum pink.

"It feels as though this room is a synthesis of our different tastes. I like simple, austere things. Jean Christophe prefers them a little more baroque. Here there are both styles," explains Erwin.

On the wall hangs an etching from the 1800s that represents Columbus's return from America. Just over a century ago, Paris was the etching capital of the world.

From the bathtub, guests can look out over the towers and pinnacles of Paris.

If the B&B was the subject of compromise, there was one thing that was never negotiable when Jean-Christophe and Erwin met: the cocker spaniel Rapsody.

"Actually, I thought it was a crazy idea hav-

ing a dog in Paris, but I had to take her too. She was part of the package – all or nothing," says Erwin.

Today he'd find it hard to live without Rapsody.

When Erwin and Rapsody relax together, they watch television. Erwin loves American television series.

"A few weeks ago we had a visit from some friends who had travelled a long way to come and see us. When they arrived, Erwin said that in half an hour he would have to leave them in order to see the latest episode of his favourite series. And he actually did it too!" Jean-Christophe tells us.

Since they moved into their little palace, they've realised what real luxury is:

"Space! Being able to invite friends home for dinner," says Erwin.

At home, he is usually responsible for the desserts. Jean-Christophe is the wizard at the starters and main courses. Although today he's the man who's going to prepare a delicious plum pie for us.

When they go out to eat it's usually round the corner to Le Restaurant de l'Homme. It's one of the best places for viewing the Eiffel Tower.

"Although their tuna tart is exquisite too," adds Jean-Christophe.

If they get over-indulgent, the couple pays a visit to the gym for a couple of hours of working out and pumping iron.

Like many other couples, this harmonises their lifestyles. Erwin, who could work all night

MOSCOW

A house with a dramatic history

MOSCOW CAN BE very hot in the summer. Today the temperature has crept well above the 30 degree mark and it feels as if the whole city is panting in the heat.

Nowhere is really cool, not even the tunnels, deep beneath the city that make up the extensive and often beautiful underground system.

In the apartment on Granatnij Lane, the windows have been opened wide in order to catch the few puffs of breeze that sometimes go by.

"I've sent my husband and children to our *dacha*, our summer house in Zarisk outside Moscow," Viktoria Kruchnina tells us when we meet in her apartment. "We're used to having air conditioning but unfortunately the system has broken down."

Some sudden drilling and banging indicates that someone, somewhere in the building, is trying to do something about the system which has gone on strike.

Viktoria offers us ice-cold rosé wine and green tea as a remedy for the heat before she starts talking about the history of the building.

"These apartments were built by the famous architect and sculptor Mitrofan Rukavisjnikov. He lived there first," she says nodding towards the house next door.

"One day, the doorbell rang and a man walked in. It was the 1930s, and the man was Lavrentij Berija, head of the Secret Police, better known to posterity as Stalin's Executioner. 'I want this apartment,' said Berija. 'You'll have to move somewhere else.'"

"Rukavisjnikov had no choice of course," says Viktoria. He was forced to move out and it later emerged that the house next door was empty.

"There was only one floor and it consisted of an empty stable," Viktoria continues. But Rukavisjnikov saw an exciting opportunity and took on the building project. Above the stables, he built a further three floors in an experimental style with beams and without supporting walls. This apartment is one of the ones that he built.

True or otherwise, such is the story told by the inhabitants of the house which stands today in one of Moscow's most attractive areas.

"That house was once the home of the Soviet Union's leader Leonid Brezhnev," says Viktoria and points diagonally across a leafy green area outside the kitchen window. It was owned by his family until just a few years ago and was very special. Among other things, it had its own water supply.

But above all, the area belongs to architects and artists.

"Many of them have always lived here," she tells us. "The poet Anna Akhmatova, for example, lived in the apartment above ours and the Architects' House is in this neighbourhood."

And just around the corner is Mala Bronnaja, where Nikolayevich meets the devil in the company of a black cat and a bloodthirsty naked woman in Bulgakov's famous novel, *The Master and Margarita*.

Viktoria and her husband Alexei Gubchenko moved here ten years ago.

"We're both doctors and met whilst reading medicine," she explains. "In reality I had no interest at all in medicine, but I come from a family with many, many doctors in it so it was simply expected of me."

Most of all, she wanted to be involved in art and design – and this interest began early.

"When I was a child, we had a big bathroom which I thought was rather boring. So I woke up one night and got out of bed. The family was extremely surprised when they went into the bathroom next morning and found that it had suddenly been decorated with stars and was full of beautiful things that I had put there."

Her career as a doctor ended when she became ill herself.

"Something took place inside me which I can't really explain, but it made me give up medicine and take up design instead."

But it wasn't without its consequences.

"I became the black sheep of the family," Viktoria laughs. "No one spoke to me for three years. My mother still tells me what a good doctor I would have been."

Viktoria has a strong personality and would probably not be happy anywhere else than in enormous, chaotic Moscow.

It's Europe's largest city, with a history filled with beauty, war, cruelty and powerful passions.

THE DEVIL'S IN
THE DETAIL

Her personality is reflected in the apartment. Only the children's room is traditional and a little untidy. Otherwise the decor is unique.

The 100 m² is completely dominated by the living room with its special choice of furniture and numerous small artefacts such as an old canary cage, statuettes, dolls, hundred year-old Russian paintings, 1930s hats and cupids which she bought in Paris.

"The devil's in the detail," quotes Viktoria delightedly.

Three sofas stand elegantly along the walls.

Over one of them hangs a painting of Viktoria herself. She poses beneath the picture for our photographer together with a large photograph of her husband and children, Victor and Elisabeth.

"And this sofa is a present from my husband," she says and points to a second one in the collection.

Two of the walls are covered in mirrors.

"It's not to make the room appear bigger, it's for the sake of the light," she explains. "Light and rhythm are the most important parts of the decor in my rooms. Unfortunately, I've been forced to place things in front of the mirrors because my guests insisted on trying to walk straight through them. I'd like to capture even more light by having a window that goes right down to the floor."

There is no television or computer in sight. There is however an ultra-modern, elegant CD player.

"I'm not keen on the kind of technology that you have to keep changing all the time," explains Viktoria. "But this particular CD player has a design that will last for several years."

Instead of normal little coffee tables, a pair of gigantic bass drums stands in front of the sofas.

"There are no beautiful coffee tables," says Viktoria firmly and with a hint of regret. "That's why I use these drums. When I deal with other designers, I ask them to show me a beautiful coffee table. It's my way of testing them. I bought the drums at a flea market."

Large, 1970s-style rice paper lamps float above everything.

"I see the apartment as my workshop," she continues. "It was designed and decorated ten years ago. At the time nobody thought it was worth having. Now the times have caught up with me, journalists come here to look, which means it's time for me to do something else.

"It's not difficult for me to get rid of things. Although the children will have to be included in the decisions too. It's their home too, after all. They grew up here. They'll probably want to keep the portrait of the sad dog that they say reminds them of Granny …"

The new decor will probably be very Russian.

"After the fall of the Soviet Union there was a tendency to look down on everything Russian", she explains. "Only foreign goods, mostly from France, were considered to be good. Now things have changed. Russians are looking for their roots and are more selective in relation to products and influences from other countries. I notice this in my work as an interior designer and in the increasing interest in Russian art."

It's still very hot out on the street. There's not a breath of wind and the guards further down the street are sweating in their uniforms. Viktoria reverses her car, a cabriolet, from the parking space.

"There are four embassies in the vicinity so it's a surprisingly safe street," she says. "I can even forget to lock the car

Only the
children's room
is traditional and
a little untidy,
otherwise
the decor
is unique.

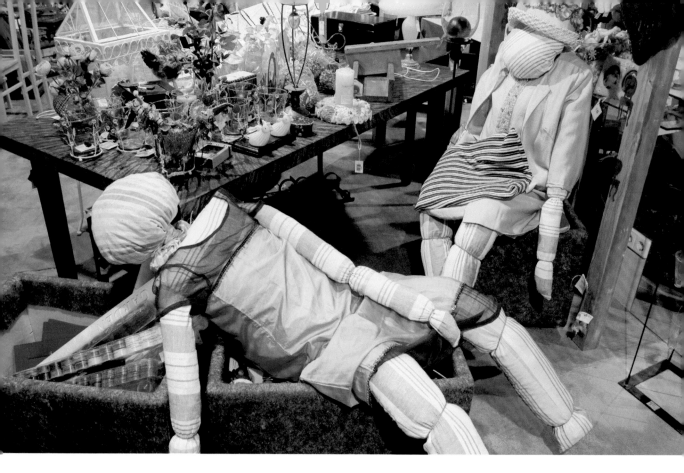

occasionally and nothing happens. Overall, Moscow feels more secure now than it did even just a year ago. Most people have lived in this neighbourhood for a very long time, so they know each other."

From the outside, there's nothing special about the house. On the contrary, it's pale yellow, with an anonymous facade and no character. Inside, there's a shabby staircase.

But the attractive position, the generous space in an otherwise extremely cramped Moscow and the fine condition of the apartment contribute to its extraordinary market value.

Viktoria owns three shops in the city centre and plans to open a fourth in the ground floor of the building where she lives. All of the shops deal

in art and design, but with a very personal touch. They mirror her own apartment, filled with forgotten things ranging from cheap jewellery to old toys. "Some people would call this kitsch, others wonder whether it's good or bad art.

"I don't ask that question," says Viktoria. "For me this is art, that's my way of looking at it. But in the same way as with my apartment, I'll soon be changing direction. This was designed several years ago. I want to continue being provocative."

Then she says goodbye, her work is calling.

Her husband Alexei turns up to replace her. He's returned to Moscow to look after his company. The children are still at the dacha.

Alexei is 38 years old, pressured but friendly, with intelligent eyes behind his glasses.

"I share my wife's interest in design," he says. "She's unbelievably creative and I think that I have something of that in me too. But two similar people in the home wouldn't work for us. So the home is her area – I put my creativity into my work. Besides, I almost always work 16–18 hours a day and I'm not at home as much as I would like to be."

Alexei is not Russian. He's a Lithuanian from Klaipeda. He came to Moscow to read medicine. Unlike his wife, there are no doctors in his family.

"None at all," he says. "My mother was a florist and my father an army officer."

In the beginning, Alexei was very successful.

"I worked with lung transplants and published 28 scientific papers on this subject," he tells

us. "But I never really felt like a doctor."

When the Soviet Union collapsed, he suddenly found himself unemployed and was forced, despite his specialist skills, to change direction completely.

"Five of us doctors set up in business together instead. Our idea was to start a business in the area of organic chemistry."

Today, Alexei runs the company alone. It has 200 employees in seven countries.

"Three of the others are now working as doctors again," he says. "Only one is a businessman, but he works in a different field now. When I retire, I'm going to write a book about what happened to our little group."

Then he too disappears into the anarchic Moscow traffic. It's late on Friday afternoon and people are hurrying home or out to the countryside. In the distance, we can hear the sound of broken chords from an electric guitar.

A rock concert is being set up in a car park between the Red Square and the Moscow River.

Next morning, Viktoria appears on Moscow television talking about hats – her own and others'.

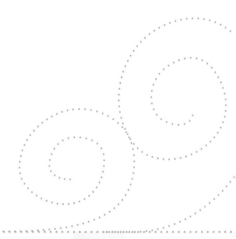

BLINI *6 portions*

25 g yeast	2 egg whites	finely chopped onion
500 ml milk	butter or margarine	finely cut gravlax
200 ml wheat flour		hard-boiled chopped eggs
200 ml buckwheat flour	**Accompaniments**	finely chopped dill
2 egg yolks	sour cream or crème fraiche	melted butter
½ tsp salt		
3 tbsp soured cream	whitefish roe	

Crumble the yeast into a bowl. Warm the milk to approx. 37 °C. Pour a little milk over the yeast and stir until dissolved.

Add wheat flour, buckwheat flour, and the rest of the milk, egg yolks and salt.

Stir until the mixture is smooth and free of lumps. Cover the bowl and allow to ferment for approx. 1 hour at room temperature.

Add the sour cream to the mixture. Whisk the egg whites until stiff and fold into the mixture immediately before cooking.

Melt a little butter and add spoonfuls of the mixture to a blini pan, pancake griddle or ordinary frying pan. Turn the blinis when they've swelled up and stiffened on the upper side.

Serve the blinis hot with accessories in small bowls.

MOSCOW · RUSSIA

Official name: Rossijskaja Federatsija/Russian Federation

Official language: Russian

Capital city: Moscow

Area: 17 million km²

Population: 143.7 million inhabitants

Population density: 8 inhabitants/km²

Currency: Rouble, RUB

Internet users: 409 per 10,000 inhabitants

UNDERGROUND

Moscow's underground is best known for its beauty. It consists of marble platforms lit with chandeliers and decorated with statues, relief, mosaics and paintings.

Construction of the system began in the 1930s with the aim of demonstrating to the world that only the best was good enough for the soviet workers and peasants.

RUSSIAN CAVIAR

Genuine caviar is a real delicacy the world over. It's also known as Rus-

sian caviar. Caviar is roe from the fish known as sturgeon which is caught in the Russian waters of the Caspian Sea, amongst other places.

Genuine caviar is categorised by the size of the roe and named after the species of sturgeon from which it comes. The most exclusive caviar is called *beluga*, whilst the type with the smallest roe is called *sevruga*.

VODKA

Vodka originated in Russia. The Russians supposedly learned the art of distilling from the Mongols during the 12th Century. In order to mask the taste of amylic alcohol, they began to experiment in the 14th Century with various flavourings such as fruits and spices. As a result, the drink became popular and was given the name vodka which means "little water".

As the drink's popularity increased, various traditions began to grow around it. If a daughter was born, a wine barrel was filled with vodka and saved until she was mar-

ried in order to celebrate the marriage with a fine, matured vodka.

During the 16th Century, adders were caught and placed live inside vodka bottles. This was to give the vodka a better taste and drinking it guaranteed a lively party … Thanks to the drink's increased popularity, the Russians began exporting it and strict laws were created in order to maintain its quality. Vodka became the world's most-consumed spirit after the beginning of the 19th Century when distillers began filtering it through charcoal. This gave it a refined and pure taste.

WARSAW

Living in constant change

ONE FINAL STEP AND WE emerge 50 years into the future. That's the distance between the worst of Communism's grey era and the beautiful modern apartment that is home to Karina Snuszka and Philip Evison.

Communism in Poland in the 1950s was a time of many negative events and when we arrive at Karina and Philip's house in Warsaw, we feel heavy-hearted. It was built in 1902 and in old photographs we can see a beautiful turn-of-the century house with a stone facade and the obligatory facade decorations.

Today, all that remains is a naked brick wall and the bolts that once held the stone plates in place.

"The house survived the Second World War," Karina tells us. But some time during the 1950s the Communists removed the whole of the facade in order to use it somewhere else.

In the staircase of the house, we can still glimpse the stolen beauty, but it's only when we step over the threshold of Karina and Philip's home that the great transformation is apparent.

This is compact living at its best. Only 60 m², with every square metre used and still there's room for some beautiful open spaces.

"My friends were very sceptical when I bought this apartment three years ago," says Karina. "It was small and dull, but I liked the atmosphere. I thought it gave out positive energy. It also had high ceilings, which I liked."

"Most Poles are still sceptical about old apartments and would rather live in modern ones. But I wanted an apartment like this. And it's also great when you get an apartment where you're free to do everything from scratch."

Karina knows her stuff. At home in Poznan in western Poland, she trained as an interior designer before starting work with a company that sold furniture.

"When the company opened an office in Warsaw I moved too," she tells us.

After arriving in Warsaw, she started her own company focusing on interior design.

"My customers are mostly men, foreign or Polish businessmen who don't have time to fix their own apartments and ask me to take care of it instead," she explains.

In her apartment, she had the opportunity to do this for herself.

"I pulled down all non-supporting walls, fixed the ceiling, laid down a new floor and moved the kitchen," she says all in one breath.

What remains now is a studio with a bedroom, living room and kitchen area. There is also a combined bathroom and shower room with toilet.

"It was important for me to have access to both," says Karina when we look into the shower room. "I use the shower every day and the bathroom when I have time to relax."

The floor of the shower is special. Instead of normal tiles, the shower floor consists of movable ceramic tiles in which the water runs down between the gaps.

I TORE
DOWN ALL
THE NON-
SUPPORT-
ING WALLS,
FIXED THE
CEILING,
PUT DOWN
NEW
FLOORS
AND
MOVED THE
KITCHEN.

From the staircase we come directly into the kitchen area and the first thing to catch our eye is the lamp which is covered in small white slips of paper.

These aren't stick-it reminders, but all kinds of greetings in different languages, Italian recipes and little love letters from Philip. Her dentist has also made a contribution: "Karina – brush your teeth after every meal!"

The colour scheme is discreet – white and grey.

"Many people don't like grey, but I think it's a pleasant neutral colour that's easy to combine with others," says Karina.

On the other hand, there are strong colours in the pictures. The only really blue colour is in a

picture hanging above the bed in the bedroom.

"Philip bought that," Karina tells us. The picture is by the famous Polish artist Walkuski and is inspired by the book *The Seagull: the story of Jonathan Livingston Seagull.*

In the window alcove is a picture of a totally different kind.

"It represents one of the seven deadly sins: gluttony," says Karina. "I met the artist Tomasz Sentowski at a casino once. He had no money with him to gamble with, so I gave him some. The next day, I got the money back – plus this painting."

The floors in the apartment are reddish-brown. The material is wood, but it's hard to discern what type.

"It's merbau, a tree that grows in Malaysia among other places and it's very durable," says Karina. "The colour is similar to a nearby mirror frame, but that's cherry."

She strokes her fingers lightly over the frame of a large mirror in the bedroom and then begins telling us her thoughts on interior design:

"We live here and now and shouldn't copy the past. Take the best of what once was and then add something new, that's a better solution."

"Poles are not particularly bold when it comes to interiors," she continues with a certain resignation in her voice. "Most continue to go for traditional heavy, dark oak. This is particularly common in the countryside where people build as if they're going to live there for perhaps 30–40 years."

"But in Warsaw it's a bit different. Here, people have more money, are more mobile and change their homes more often."

Karina gets many of her interior design impulses from her trips abroad.

"I used to do Polish folk dancing for many years," she tells us. "We travelled everywhere – China, Canada, Israel and every country in Europe. I got to see a lot."

She guides us on to the bathroom.

"Teak," she says with a hint of pride in her voice. "The bathtub is also built into a sort of

The washing machine is hidden behind a curtain in the shower room, but where is the vacuum cleaner?

stone which means that the water stays hot for an hour. Very pleasant when you're lying there reading, or if you just want to enjoy the bath for longer. The floor tiles are of the same material."

The telephone rings and Karina disappears. While she's talking, we take the opportunity to inspect the kitchen more closely. It's German with a modern hob and most of the equipment built in behind discreet cupboard doors. Both Karina and Philip are interested in cooking. She's mostly interested in Italian cuisine – a memory of her time as an architecture student in Perugia:

"Two things were fantastic at that time," Karina tells us when she's finished her telephone conversation. "One was that much of the teaching could take place out on the street where there were so many examples. The other was the food.

I used to look over the cooks' shoulders to see how they did things."

Most things in the kitchen are easy to find; it's just the dishwasher which avoids detection. But we eventually find it under the central unit which also houses the dining table.

"I couldn't find anywhere else to put it," says Karina. The drain is built into the floor.

What do you do with household equipment when you live in such a compact space? The washing machine is hidden behind a curtain in the shower room, but where is the vacuum cleaner?

"Here," says Karina finally.

The mirror in the bedroom, the one with the cherry wood frame, also turns out to be a cupboard door. Inside are fifty pairs of

shoes in a rack and other things sorted in boxes marked for summer and winter use. And even the vacuum cleaner is there, well hidden away!

The apartment's balcony is not large and looks as if it's going to fall onto the street at any moment.

"Don't worry," laughs Karina. "I had it reinforced with steel girders when I moved in here."

From the balcony you can see a street reminiscent of French and Italian streets with their four-storey houses, badly parked cars, people, noisy voices and the little greengrocer's shop opposite.

To the right, you can catch a glimpse of Plac Konstytucji – Constitution Square – a display of social realist art with massive buildings and three sturdy streetlights that were the height of fashion in Communist Poland in 1952.

You can't see it from the balcony, but in the next block is the main street, Aleja Niepodłeglosci. This was where the Jewish pianist Wladyslaw Szpilman had his last hiding place from the Nazis in the winter of 1944–45. His fate was later the subject of the film *The Pianist*, directed by another famous Pole – Roman Polanski.

The apartments in Karina and Philip's house are mostly privately owned, but some are still in state ownership and rented by those who live there. However, the actual building is privately owned. Prices are high and rising at an astonishing rate.

A year ago, Philip Evison entered Karina's life and apartment.

"He quickly declared his love, both for me and my espresso machine," laughs Karina. "Then he bombarded me, in the modern way, with text messages in which he said that he had a mass of inter-

esting projects under way that would suit me. But I felt that he really had something else in mind."

Philip has an international background with a Canadian father and a Polish mother. He grew up in Belgium and the USA. He's a political science graduate but works as an estate agent.

Karina wants to show us some of her favourite places so she takes us out for a tour of the town.

"We'll have to hurry before things disappear," she jokes. "This is what makes Warsaw different from many other cities. Everything is changing very fast at the moment. If you return to Rome after a year, most things look the same as they did before. Here, it can be completely different."

The first stop is a clothes shop with garments from Poland's fashion king, Maciej Zien and here you can guarantee that they're *Made in Poland*. Everything is made by the shop's twelve seamstresses.

In the same building is Utopia, one of the city's in-places whose clientele is a carefully selected circle of people.

During the War, Warsaw was almost completely destroyed on several occasions: the German attack in 1939, the Jewish ghetto uprising in 1943 and the Warsaw uprising in 1944. After the last uprising, Hitler decided that as much of the city as possible should be destroyed.

When the German troops finally withdrew, 85 percent of Warsaw lay in ruins. During the years that followed, the Poles made heroic efforts to rebuild their capital. With the help of old

NEON! GLISTENING ASPHALT! Yellow taxis, street vendors and death-defying bike couriers. Eateries and people from every corner of the earth. Steaming drains and buildings that stretch skywards.

And everywhere, an energy so intense you can almost touch it.

The image of Downtown Manhattan is familiar to hundreds of millions of people, from films, television and visits. An inviting, inspiring and for many perhaps slightly frightening urban chaos. This is the city that never sleeps, but for Jonathan, Lauren and Greta Schloss it is, above all, Home.

For the past few years, the little family has lived in Greenwich Village. They have the most classic street in Manhattan both as an address and a view: Broadway, the old Indian trail which cuts diagonally across the entire island.

"When I moved to New York in 1988, it seemed the best place for me in terms of both architecture and art," says Jonathan.

He comes from Vancouver in Canada, but now both his mother and brother live within walking distance and he can even walk to his own architect's studio.

The couple's enthusiasm over living in the middle of this cauldron, in a place with roots, is unmistakable. As real New Yorkers, the family live south of 14th Street, on lower Manhattan, where the city first began to grow after Dutch colonists bought the island from the Indians in 1626.

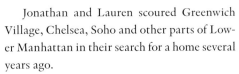

Jonathan and Lauren scoured Greenwich Village, Chelsea, Soho and other parts of Lower Manhattan in their search for a home several years ago.

Having looked at several hundred apartments, they saw this building. They liked its open position near the church; just on a small curve in Broadway and close to the student life of New York University. They asked their estate agent to tell them if there was anything on sale.

Suddenly, a two-room co-op apartment of almost 70 m² and with views in two directions became available on the second floor. In one direction, there is the bustle of Broadway, Grace Church with its churchyard and blossoming magnolia trees, and in the other, 11th Street with a view of a large tree to the west. Jonathan saw the potential immediately.

Grace Episcopal Church was designed by architect James Renwick in the British neo-Gothic style in the 1840s. The church became something of a qualifying test for Renwick, who gradually gained the confidence to design more famous buildings including the Smithsonian Institute in Washington DC and Saint Patrick's Cathedral on Fifth Avenue in Manhattan's Midtown area.

Several decades later, the architect had both his home and his office in a beautifully ornamented property near Grace Church – a house that he designed himself in the 1880s.

"I like the idea that he could sit here and look out at the church that he built as a young man," says Jonathan of his predecessor as he looks out over a contemporary version of the same view.

By demolishing several walls, making the bedroom into a living room and painting it white, white, white, they created a light, airy apartment; a real compact living space in which every surface is used to the full.

"In some ways, I've been inspired by Japanese home architecture. I wanted to include two small, efficient sleeping spaces and have the rest as open as possible," explains Jonathan.

He shows us how a sliding door separates Greta's little nursery corner from the parents' bedroom, and how their double-bed can be folded up into the wall so that there's more free floorspace.

"It only takes ten seconds to fold down the bed. And even Greta can push the door aside!"

Everywhere in the apartment there are smart solutions invented by the couple. The wardrobes in the hall for example, deep enough to hold double rows of clothes, and the shelves that are set into the bathroom walls.

So that the home does not feel overloaded, all of their books – almost a ton of thick volumes reflecting the family's professional interest in art, photography and architecture – have been concentrated on a single wall of bookshelves in the living room.

And they've used other space-saving tricks: pots and other cooking utensils are hung on walls or from the ceiling, the television has a flat screen and lighting is through spotlights set in the ceiling.

"One good thing about living in a small space is that you have to prioritise what you need," says Lauren, but admits they've still been forced to store a lot of clothes and other items at her parents' home.

And her husband quotes the Canadian author Robertson Davies from his book *The Rebel Angels* where he says "too much cleanliness is an enemy to creation".

"That's my favourite quote. We like it modern and spartan at home, but it must not be sterile."

What characterises their minimalist home is all personal objects, each one with its own story. The living room carpet is patterned with graphic maps of Venice, New Delhi and other world cities; this was originally designed for the Windows on the World restaurant on the 107th floor of the World Trade Center' North Tower. For well-known and tragic reasons the piece that Jonathan bought is probably the only piece of that carpet still existing.

Most of the couple's many paintings and photographs are by artist friends – except for a collection of watercolour works, prominently placed in the living room. These were painted by Greta, who will soon be three years old.

Some of the furniture comes from Jonathan's childhood home, others are design history classics that the couple have collected. There are also some unusual objects, like the small mass-produced Korean table that the couple bought cheaply during their honeymoon in Hawaii. Or

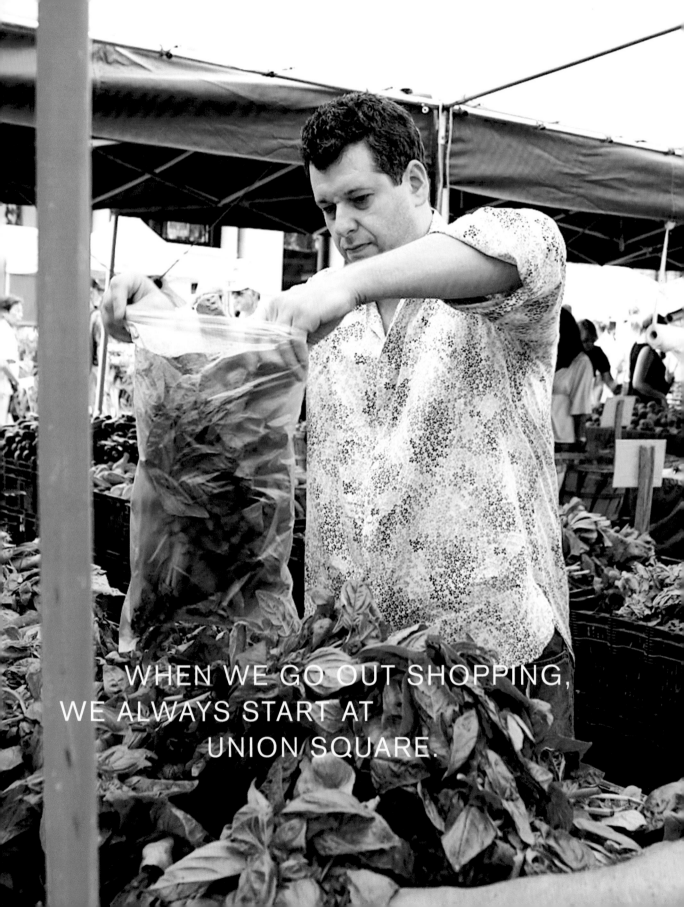

WHEN WE GO OUT SHOPPING, WE ALWAYS START AT UNION SQUARE.

JONATHAN AND LAUREN'S CAESAR SALAD

2–4 persons

2 romaine lettuces
4 cloves of garlic
1 tsp flake salt
2 tsp freshly squeezed lemon juice
1 tsp Worcestershire sauce
2–4 anchovies
black pepper
100 ml good quality olive oil
1 egg
100–200 ml Parmesan cheese

CROUTONS
some slices of crusty bread
4 cloves garlic
200 ml olive oil
50 g butter

Use the fine, light leaves from the romaine lettuces. Tear them into 3–5 cm long pieces. Rinse and dry the lettuce.

Using a mortar and pestle, crush the garlic cloves with salt into a soft pulp. Stir in lemon juice and Worcestershire sauce. Rinse anchovies and mash them into the garlic paste. Season with black pepper. Allow dressing to stand for a while.

Add olive oil by pouring in a thin drizzle whilst stirring vigorously with a whisk or fork.

Cube the slices of bread. Fry garlic cloves in olive oil until golden, approx. 10 min. Melt butter. Filter oil, cover croutons with the oil and melted butter.

Roast croutons in the oven on greased paper for approximately 20 min. at 200 °C.

Whisk the egg and mix it with the lettuce leaves.

Mix in croutons followed by dressing. Season with pepper. Mix in grated parmesan.

Serve with grilled meat or other dishes.

the 1960s stereo with amplifier that Jonathan found amongst some rubbish and which he repaired himself after ordering spare parts from Russia.

Other objects that leave their stamp on the home are Jonathan's collection of film-roll containers from the 1940s and old ice cream scoops.

The big step forward in the apartment happened when the dividing wall between kitchen and living room was pulled down. This created a giant window looking out over the church and Broadway. Now, instead of a wall, there's a sturdy work surface with gas hob where Jonathan and Lauren often enjoy cooking in the company of friends and acquaintances.

"Yes, we enjoy food, both cooking it and eating it! And we have the best view in the apartment when we're standing in the kitchen. Many people think it's noisy to live as close to the street as we do, but it's actually quite nice to be part of the urban landscape."

Only a few blocks away lies Union Square. Growers and small-scale producers come here from upstate New York to Manhattan with organically grown fresh vegetables, fruit, bread, cheese, jam, preserves and flowers.

"When we go shopping, we always start at Union Square," Lauren tells us. "Having a market square so near to us is actually the best thing about living here! Particularly from May to October."

Every weekday morning Lauren, who teaches art, takes the car and drives across Williamsburg Bridge to her job at the Queens Museum of Art. Otherwise the streams of traffic are usually travelling in the opposite direction in the morning, towards Manhattan and then back out towards the dormitory towns in the afternoon. The museum building in which she works also contains several exciting layers of New York's dynamic history.

This is where the city had its pavilion in the 1939 world exhibition – and for several years after the Second World War, the museum housed the United Nations' General Assembly before the UN's present headquarters were built in Manhattan at the end of the 1940s.

Lauren is not as convinced as her husband that Manhattan, and in particular Greenwich Village, is the only place on earth to live. She could imagine buying a somewhat larger home, in Brooklyn for example or the neighbouring state of New Jersey, as many other New York families do when they have children.

But even the most pleasant areas have high property prices and the Schloss family do have the opportunity to get away from the urban bustle by visiting Lauren's parents in New Jersey during weekends and holidays. No matter how loyal to Manhattan many of its residents might be, most try to get away from the city sometimes, just for a change.

JOHANNES

BURG

A dream house full of love

It's trendy, cosmopolitan, socially rich and eternally sunny.

Seen from high above, Johannesburg gives the impression of a metropolis somewhere in the American south. High office blocks in the centre and endless villa suburbs with tree-lined avenues and bright blue swimming pools. Major motorways create intricate circles in every direction.

There is one significant difference, however.

The massive slag heaps like great yellowing cowpats are spread out directly to the south of the city centre and farther out, east and west of Johannesburg's patchwork of suburbs.

The slag heaps, which are disappearing as they are recycled with new technology, reveal the origins of the city: gold.

The gold rush began 130 years ago. At that time Johannesburg was nothing more than bumpy savannah. Now it's a city of six million inhabitants with enormous private palaces and appalling slums virtually side by side.

Johannesburg is a city filled with immigrants. They've come from near and far over several generations. A melting-pot of people like Xhosa, Sotho, Zulu and Tswana. Followed by Portuguese, Dutch, English, Malays, Indians, Chinese, Scots, Germans and the odd Scandinavian.

Added to this are an increasing number of people from Zimbabwe, Malawi, Congo and

others who live in the country illegally.

Some are looking for power and wealth, but most are just looking for a job.

Audrey, 36, and Ivo, 37, belong to the happy band who came to Africa's New York, this city of hope and opportunity, because it suited them.

They have quite voluntarily put down roots in one of the world's most crime-ridden cities. This is a city in which foreigners are advised to stay away from the city centre and stay in their hotel rooms after darkness falls.

What was it that drove them here? The answer, as usual, has a personal dimension.

Audrey and Ivo met in 1994 via a mutual friend when they were both studying in Toronto, Canada. It was definitely love at first sight, but when it was time to choose, they were each drawn to their own homelands.

Audrey, who is the daughter of a South African freedom fighter and consequently grew up in Exile in Tanzania, had a clear sense of direction that she could not suppress.

When she'd completed her studies, she simply had to set foot in her homeland for the first time.

Ivo, the son of a German diplomat, spent his teenage years in Stockholm and wanted to spread his wings at home in Germany.

So Audrey travelled to South Africa alone. She arrived in Johannesburg at the end of 1995, a year after Nelson Mandela had been sworn in as president.

Living apart for a long period and being so far from each other was impractical.

Ivo gave in and took a job in South Africa through the German consultancy company that he worked for.

"When we were looking for a house, there were three conditions that had to be met. We had to fall in love with it; and it had to have a swimming pool

and a tennis court," Ivo tells us.

It took them three years to find their dream house in the suburb of Parktown West, close to Johannesburg's city and Wits University.

They bought it at the right time, three years ago. Since then, prices in Johannesburg have doubled or tripled.

Ivo meets us at one of the two electronic gates to the property which lies in the grand old mine owners' quarter.

As is customary in middle-class Johannesburg suburbs, almost all of the houses are hidden behind high walls. From the street, you can never really see what's behind the walls.

"We fell for this house immediately. It was our dream house. I was ecstatic over it. We had space and a large garden," says Ivo.

The house is unusual in may ways. It's a piece of architectural history, designed by the South African architect Bernard Cooke. He moved in here himself in 1952, when the house's good points were the subject of a newspaper article.

It's not hard to understand why Cooke's house was, and still is, special.

It's highly unusual for Johannesburg, built in a modernist French or Italian villa style. It stands out from all the other houses in Parktown, with its straight lines, clean surfaces, white walls and big windows.

Parktown also has many other interesting houses, but older in style; old colonial villas built in solid stone, where the mining barons once lived, and more conventional officials' houses from the early 1920s.

Audrey and Ivo's house has no neo-classical pillars or heavy, carved oak doors. The front door is discrete, almost Scandinavian in its modesty.

The hall on the other hand is made to impress, with a broad,

A melting-pot of people like Xhosa, Sotho, Zulu and Tswana. Followed by Portuguese, Dutch, English, Malays, Indians, Chinese, Scots, Germans and the odd Scandinavian.

mighty staircase to the upper storey and palatial, high ceiling. Inside the entrance, on a desk, stands a sculpture. A three-headed cow in plastic with a round photograph of some black teenage boys. They're standing in a row at an initiation ceremony. A mixture of modern art and traditional culture.

"We buy what we like, and that can take time. There isn't really any thought behind it. We don't go looking around, we buy when something crops up. We usually discuss things back and forth, but we really have very similar tastes," says Ivo.

Audrey has also arrived home from work. She was head-hunted last year by a large life insurance company and since the beginning of the year she's been the company's first black personnel manager.

Three year-old Zoya, a cute little thing with a mop of curly hair, has taken charge of her mother Audrey.

Normally she stays at home with the housekeeper, Violet, during the day, but she's also driven around to various activities by an au pair a few times a week. Next year, she'll begin at the German playschool down the hill.

Audrey and Ivo represent the new South Africa. A country where apartheid is still in people's consciousness, but where the generation coming out onto the labour market has few or only vague memories of it.

Ivo says that the couple have encountered no hostility since they, a white guy and a black girl, moved into what was an established "white" area. Some little things come across, such as Audrey being more concerned with how her black staff are feeling than the older neighbours are, but there is no open racism.

The same goes amongst the black people; Ivo might get jibes that he shouldn't steal "our girls", but nothing more.

At work, Audrey has had confrontations with strong racist overtones.

"When I was working on one of my first consultancy assignments with a mining company in a small town, the boss whom I was supposed to advise said to me 'here comes Nelson Mandela's children's fund'."

He said this implying that she was black and young.

"He refused to work with me, but got fired," smiles Audrey sweetly.

Her integrity shines through and she's smart, which was a devastating combination for a mine manager of the old school.

"She's a front-of-the-classroom type," says Ivo, and it's not hard to imagine Audrey waving her arm and shouting "Miss, Miss! I know, I know!" when she went to the American School in Nairobi.

Ivo describes himself as a typical back-of-the-classroom type.

This gives us a clue as to who is responsible for the scrupulous order evident in the home. There's not a sign of any untidiness.

Ivo, who wears an anarchist symbol around his neck, is responsible for the clever and at times expansive decor concepts; Audrey for the implementation. At least, that is what she says.

Sometimes they can't make up their minds, like when they took home three paintings on trial by the well-known British painter, Robert Hodgins, who is now based in South Africa. They ended up buying all three.

The three brightly-coloured naive paintings now dominate the living room to the right of the hallway. One hangs by the hearth, another leans against the wall and the third has pride of place over the piano.

"I still haven't hammered in a single nail, after three years. Partly because we haven't got much to hang up, partly because of laziness," says Ivo.

The living room is sparingly furnished with two sofas in straight lines. A Senufo bed, an antique bed carved in wood from the Ivory Coast, stands behind one of the sofas.

Large French windows lead out onto the generous, sloping garden.

We sit down in the adjoining dining room. It has the character of an outdoor space with thick green climbing plants growing outside the windows that take up the whole wall.

Along the whole of the long wall runs a serving table on terracotta tiles – a small but important change made by Audrey and Ivo.

Having good serving facilities is important in Johannesburg, a town where the middle class's social life is largely based on holding large private parties.

Johannesburg, situated 1600 metres above sea-level, has an ideal climate for parties. The sun is almost always shining and it's generally dry with little rain. However, during the summer, there can be gigantic storms over the Johannesburg hills, with dramatic lightning strikes shaking the ground, followed by giant hail; but the sun soon comes out again. Johannesburg has numerous theatres, music venues and restaurants of all kinds and a cultural fusion like few other cities in the world today.

The latest big attraction is a permanent exhibition on human origins – *The Cradle of Humankind* – a short distance outside the town. Johannesburg's surrounding areas have some of the oldest remnants of human life in the world.

But most things take place in people's homes.

The desire for a rich social life is also the key to the architecture of the house. The living room, dining room and indeed every room other than the kitchen, hall and various extensions all face towards the sloping, generously proportioned garden.

Near the living room is an enormous jacaranda tree which almost swallows up the whole front of the house. The previous owners tried to stop its root-development which was threatening to force its way through the parquet floor. Whether their efforts were effective, only time will tell.

Below the grass slope there is a pool on one side, surrounded by a fence. On the other are some typical imported trees such as poplar, mulberry, camphor and lemon. Behind the greenery is a trampoline for Zoya to jump on and right at the end of the garden is the tennis court.

Violet, the live-in housekeeper, has also had a fair share of renovation to her accommodation. Walls have been taken down and her hut is now a cottage with modern bathroom and kitchenette.

The kitchen was renovated when Audrey and Ivo moved in. Cherry-wood doors, black granite work surfaces and a large refrigerator. High up on one of the short walls is a bell with stars that shake so that the housekeeping staff can see which room needs attending to. This is one detail which is more characteristic of Parktown's mining baron houses than of this particular house and its new owners.

The bedrooms are on the upper floor. All the rooms are in a row with a view over the garden and the valley below.

Zoya's room comes first, neatly furnished only with children's furniture. Then a room in the middle which is used as a study. The third one, on the far corner of the corridor is Audrey and Ivo's light bedroom.

Compromises have been made in order to accommodate everything. The entrance of the house faces what was once a service alley.

Visitors can't park there. They have to park out on the street and walk around 50 metres, or park

round the corner, go in through a little door down in the garden and then cross the tennis court.

For this, the laser alarm in the garden has to be shut off. Otherwise, the security company will turn out in response. Fortunately, the family have not suffered any break-ins to the house, only petty thefts from the garden.

"It's a part of life here, and of course it's stressful. We live in a fool's paradise with enormous social gulfs and material differences. Poverty is the cause of this. I do what I can by helping everyone in our surroundings who is in need of support," says Audrey.

She is well aware of the various huge barriers that she has succeeded in overcoming. On one day

Audrey may be sitting in a management meeting with some of the country's leading businesspeople. The next, she may be at a party with relatives helping to slaughter a cow.

For Audrey Mothupi there is no contradiction in this. It simply adds a little spice to life. It is the change in society that is the oxygen in Audrey and Ivo's lives.

"We're wondering what we're going to do next. We probably won't stay in Johannesburg forever. We need to experience other things too. We're thinking about Berlin actually," says Audrey and smiles archly at Ivo.

But can they bear to leave their happy, almost Californian Johannesburg lifestyle?

It won't be easy, but it might work.

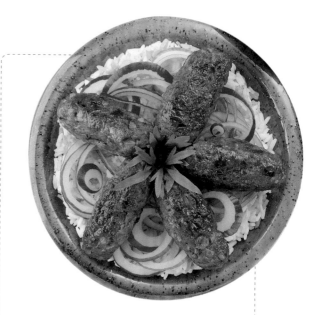

Sosaties

4 persons

400 g minced lamb	1 tsp lemon juice
1 onion	½ tsp coriander
6 dried apricots	½ tsp fenugreek
1 tsp salt	1 tsp sugar
1 pinch of black pepper	

Heat oven to 275 °C. Peel and finely chop onion. Finely chop the apricots.

Mix the mince with onions, apricots, salt, pepper, lemon juice, coriander, fenugreek and sugar. Stir until mixture is smooth.

Shape the mince into long rolls. Push a wet wooden skewer through the length of the roll. Grease pan with oil and lay in the lamb kebabs.

Place the kebabs in the upper part of the oven and turn them several times during roasting until they are golden brown all over, 5–10 min. Alternatively, grill the kebabs over charcoal on a barbecue.

Serve with boiled rice or pitta bread and salad.

JOHANNESBURG • SOUTH AFRICA

Official name:
Republic of South Africa

Official languages: Zulu, Xhosa,
Afrikaans, English and others

Capital city: Pretoria

Area: 1.2 million km²

Population: 47.3 million inhabitants

Population density:
36 inhabitants/km²

Currency: rand, ZAR

Internet users:
682 per 10,000 inhabitants

WINE PRODUCER

In 1654 the first vines were planted in
South Africa by the Dutch governor
Jan Van Riebeck. This was the beginning of South Africa's long and very
successful history of wine production.

Today, South Africa is the world's
sixth-largest wine producer.

ANIMAL LIFE

South Africa is the home of the
world's largest land mammal, the
African elephant. It's also home to
the world's tallest animal, the giraffe,
the world's fastest animal, the chee-
tah, and the world's largest bird, the
ostrich.

It's also home to 900 different
species of bird, in other words, 10 %
of all bird species in the world. There
are more species of wild creature
in South Africa than in the whole of
North and South America, Europe
and Asia put together!

THREE CAPITALS

South Africa has three capitals. The
legislative capital is Cape Town,
where the country's parliament sits.
Pretoria is the administrative capital
and Bloemfontein is the legal capital.

RICH NATURAL ASSETS

The world's largest diamond was
discovered in Transvaal in South
Africa. It was named the Cullinan
diamond after Sir Thomas Cullinan
who founded the mine in which it was
discovered.

The original size of the diamond
was 3,106 carats and it had a weight
of 621.2 g. It has since been cut and
polished into 9 large and 96 smaller
jewels, of which the largest, the great
Star of Africa, is 530 carats or 106 g.
It is now part of the English Crown
Jewels.

RAINBOW NATION

Archbishop Desmond Tutu once
called South Africa the Rainbow Na-
tion of Africa, in reference to its many
different cultures, languages, traditions and skin colours.

MUMBAI

Duplex apartment à la *My Fair Lady*

WE CLIMB INTO ONE OF THE city's small yellow and black taxis in Mumbai harbour. It's the middle of the day, traffic is moving and we soon reach Chowpatty Beach.

We drive past the beach, which by sunset will be filled with strolling couples, families and young people.

Our journey continues up Walkeshwar Road towards the high apartment blocks at the top of Malabar Hill, home of the rich in Mumbai.

The taxi drives down the narrow three-lane Mount Pleasant, passing the City Administrator's residence before stopping at Dorshan, a secluded residential area.

The uniformed security guard shows us the way to the lifts and we take one up to the ninth floor. From there, the staircase continues up towards the luxurious roof apartment where Mr. and Mrs. Merchant live.

Sabira Merchant opens the door and welcomes us. After a short conversation she excuses herself:

"I'm sorry but today has been very busy and I'm running behind schedule. This evening I'm going to be toastmaster at a Rotary Club meeting. I have to go over my speech and prepare myself. Look around and make yourself at home. We can have a chat later."

It's a magnificent apartment dominated by a large open space which greets you at the front door. Immediately to the right is a modern kitchen with every conceivable facility.

A counter separates kitchen from dining room and there is room for at least 12 people around its circular glass dining table. The rest is the living room with white sofas and armchairs and there is a raised floor area with an office, a desk, a bar and a door to the guest toilet. Furniture and fittings blend together in a perfect union of colour and form.

The walls on both sides of the apartment are taken up by large windows and furthest away is a door leading to the bedroom and two identical "his" and "hers" bathrooms.

The largest room has a sloping ceiling with a height of at least fifteen feet. In the centre is a spiral staircase leading to another floor; up here is a library and a corridor leading to a combined reading and guest room. Some of the family servants are quietly at work, arranging furniture and sorting books on bookshelves.

A fantastic surprise is in store behind one of the doors off the corridor: a roof terrace with a 360° panoramic view of the whole of Mumbai.

The terrace has two levels linked by a spiral staircase. At one end is a little kitchen with open ovens and grills, all of which are covered over because of the Monsoon season.

Sabira is elegantly dressed in preparation for the evening. She's a well-known name and face in Mumbai's social circles.

Sabira is a highly respected theatre actress and during the 1970s, she appeared in a long-running Indian television series.

Thanks to her fluent English and perfect pronunciation, Sabira (as well as being an actress) teaches lecturing technique, diction and stage performance; she has helped such people as India's Miss Universe and Miss World to achieve success.

"I grew up in Mumbai. I have seen the city change so much over the last 60 years that it feels as though Mumbai has grown up with me. Despite its size, I know every street and every corner of the city and feel proud to be a citizen of Mumbai. I identify with it," says Sabira.

"If there's anywhere in India with a fast pulse, it's here. I like the pace of life and the stress. I wouldn't want to be anywhere else. Of course, Mumbai is a hard nut to crack, but I like to work and if you work hard, Mumbai will reward you. Mumbai has given me a good life and now it feels more and more as if it's time for me to give something back. One way of doing this is to help the Rotary Club and other similar associations to collect money for charitable purposes," Sabira continues.

One social project that Sabira is committed to is Project Mainstream, which is intended to keep Mumbai's young people off the streets by creating jobs and apprenticeships for them. It's a chance for the city's underprivileged people to begin climbing up Mumbai's golden ladder to success and happiness.

Unfortunately, our conversation with Sabira is a short one. Her car is waiting to take her to the evening's Rotary meeting and early next day she is flying to Chandigarh in northern India for a three-day workshop. Chotu, Sabira's husband has arrived home and we agree to meet again the next morning.

Chotu has built up a very successful company that manufactures glass bottles and ampoules for the pharmaceutical industry. He is now semi-retired and works from home. He only visits the office for a few days each month.

When we meet again and stand on the terrace, Chotu begins talking about his home:

"This started at the end of the 1950s. My father had a chronic illness and our doctor often had to visit our home. One day, I drove the doctor home. At that time he lived here in Dorshan. It was all newly built and I'd never been here before. I liked the building and when I heard that the two top floors were for sale, I decided to buy them. That was in 1959. I had the apartments decorated and on our wedding day, 25th February 1960, I brought Sabby to our new home; we've lived in Dorshan ever since."

"Subsequently, we had the opportunity to build an extra floor on the roof. We happened to meet the Italian architect, Eugeno Montevari, who was working on a project in India. We commissioned him to design this apartment," continues Chotu after a short pause.

"Sabby had always wanted a garden and a terrace and I knew she loved duplex apartments having seen one in *My Fair Lady*. So I asked Montevari to make our home into a duplex apartment. I also made sure that the walls were thick enough to withstand the monsoon weather," Chotu concludes.

The sea, monsoons and high air humidity mean that many homes in Mumbai have a problem with damp. Chotu tells us about a friend who lives near the water in Walkeshwar Road who has to change the hinges on his doors every year because of corrosion from salt water and winds.

We look north towards a densely populated area with skyscrapers and high-rise residential buildings.

"When we moved here, that was forest," Chotu recalls.

Fifty years ago, Malabar Hill was covered in forest. There were only villas and bungalows here, built in the colonial style and spread out among the trees. During the hottest months of the year, the people who lived and worked down in the city sought refuge on Malabar Hill where there was shade and the temperature was a few degrees lower.

Throughout history, Mumbai has been a magnet to people from all over India and from distant places. The city became the commercial hub of India, the city of dreams to which people came seeking happiness and success.

The need for land on Mumbai's narrow peninsula increased and the city sprawled into the sea and onto the hills to find space for everyone living there.

Now Mumbai is growing faster than ever. Thousands of people arrive here every week. They come in the hope of fleeing their past and realis-

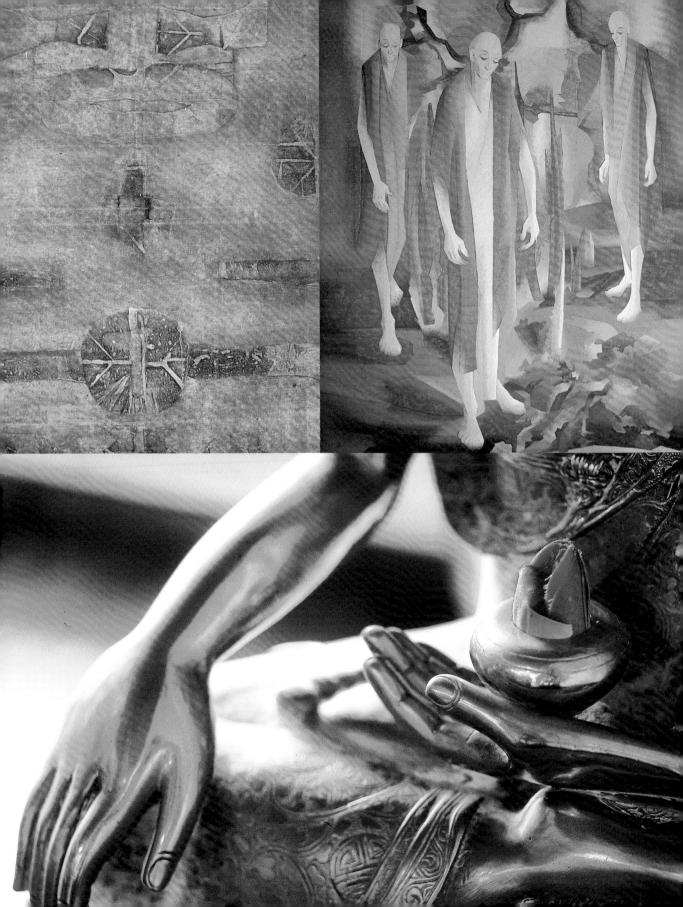

ing their dreams in this place. Despite the fact that many end up on the streets or in one of the city's many slum areas, few of them want to leave the city.

Mumbai's population is now 18 million and is expected to reach 25 million by 2015. There are few places on earth where so many people live crammed together in such a small area. It is estimated that in some places in Mumbai there are almost 400,000 people per km^2!

Chotu points at the new high-rise buildings in Worli and Parel where young middle-class Indians are moving in.

Beyond them and out of sight is Dharavi, Asia's biggest slum area. Even further away are Bollywood and Bandra, Juhu and Vasova where many of the film stars live.

Improved borrowing facilities have made it easier for the middle class to buy their homes. But houses in Mumbai aren't cheap, particularly in attractive areas like Malabar Hill.

We walk around the apartment and Chotu continues to tell us about their thinking at the time they renovated it:

"We had the possibility of choosing an open plan solution. Our three children had grown up and moved out, so we didn't need as many bedrooms or common areas any more."

The apartment is over 300 m^2 and the terrace is 90 m^2.

"The terrace is a great source of pleasure for us. The cook can use the kitchen up there and all the cooking smells disappear into the open air. During the dry season we hold parties – we hire

in catering firms and light the outdoor barbecues. We can accommodate over a hundred guests."

When the couple eat at home, Sabira sometimes cooks in the main kitchen:

"She makes the best pasta I've ever eaten. You won't taste better, even in Italy or anywhere else in Europe or the USA. We often go out to eat – with friends, in clubs or restaurants. Nowadays you can eat food from all over the world in Mumbai. One of my favourite restaurants is the Royal China," Chotu tells us and then answers questions about his favourite food:

"My favourite dish? It must be Paya – the feet of a goat or lamb prepared in the traditional Muslim way which is common in Gujarat."

We discuss the Objets d'art in the apartment. Standing by the front door is one of the favour-ites, a 300 year old wooden sculpture from Rajas-than; this was a housewarming present. However, most of the items were created by modern Indian artists, including a sculpture from driftwood by Ved Prakash and paintings by Hussain, Gaitonde and Sabawallah.

"We're not collectors in the real sense of the word. We buy art from art markets and galleries. We buy the pieces that we like. We don't see them as investments," Chotu tells us.

"But of course, some of them have increased substantially in value. For example, we bought two paintings by Gaitonde about 40 years ago and didn't pay a great deal for them. Gaitonde is no longer alive and he wasn't a prolific artist. To-day his paintings are priceless," says Chotu.

The Merchant family like to travel the world:

"I get restless several times a year. We've had the opportunity to travel and the only part of the world I have never visited is South America. New York is an obvious destination since our daughter lives there with her family. Sabby and I were considering going to live in New York, so we stayed there for a few months, but then we began to miss Mumbai so we came home again. I missed our friends and realised that we belonged in Mumbai. Of course, one relevant factor is that we can live a comfortable life in India with servants, cooks and chauffeurs in a way that we couldn't anywhere else."

We take our leave and ask Chotu to thank Sabira for us:

"Yes, I'll do that," says Chotu smiling warmly. "I miss her a lot and I'm already longing for her to come home again."

CHICKEN JALFREZI

4 portions

2 table spoons curry powder
50 ml vegetable oil
1 tsp whole cumin
1 tsp brown mustard seeds
½ tsp turmeric
1 table spoon finely chopped garlic
1 table spoon grated ginger
600 g chicken fillets in pieces
1 thinly sliced red or yellow onion
1 finely sliced red or green paprika
2 sliced green chillies
3 tomatoes
2 table spoons chopped fresh coriander
2 tsp garam masala
salt
1 lemon in segments for garnishing

Place curry powder and 1 table spoon water in a small cup and mix well to an even paste.

Heat oil in a wok or frying pan. Add cumin and mustard seeds and fry at medium heat for 30 seconds. Add turmeric and fry mixture for 15 seconds.

Add garlic and ginger and toss mixture on medium heat for 30 seconds. Add chicken pieces. Increase heat, turning ingredients constantly for 5 minutes.

Add onion, paprika and chilli and fry for approx. 5 min. on medium heat.

Scald, peel and chop tomatoes. Add tomatoes, coriander, garam masala and salt. Fry for 5 min. stirring continuously. If the ingredients catch, add two table spoons of water and lightly scrape the bottom of the pan.

Place on a serving dish and garnish with lemon segments.

MUMBAI · INDIA

Official name:
Bhārat (hindi), Republic of India

Official languages: Hindi, English

Capital city: New Delhi

Area: 3.2 million km²

Population: 1,087 million inhabitants

Population density:
340 inhabitants/km²

Currency: Indian rupee, INR

Internet users:
175 per 10,000 inhabitants

MUMBAI

The name Mumbai comes from the mother goddess Mumbadevi and can be divided up into *Mumba*, the name of the goddess and *Aai* which means mother. The city was called Mumbai until the 1500s when the Portuguese changed its name to Bom Bahia which means "good harbour".

When the British empire later took over India, they wanted to anglicise the name and the city was called Bombay. Since 1996, the city has once more been called Mumbai.

BOLLYWOOD

Mumbai is the centre of the Indian film industry. All of the Indian languages have their own film centres. In Bollywood, Mumbai's film centre, films are made in Hindi. Films are characterised by lots of music and dance and clear differences between good and evil. A typical Bollywood film is *Dev-*

das, the story of two lovers who are kept apart due to arranged marriages. The tale is so popular that it has been made into a film on several occasions during the 20th Century.

In 2004, 946 films were produced in Bollywood, equivalent to more than two films a day!

LANGUAGES

The biggest official languages in India are Hindi and English. But there are a further 14 languages in the country that could also be classed as official. This is because many of the states in India have their borders drawn precisely on the grounds of the language spoken there.

Even the ancient classical language of Sanskrit has official status in the country. In addition, there are many different languages and dialects. It is reckoned there are 300–400 of these.

THE SACRED COW

There are several reasons why the cow is considered sacred in India. One is that the cow is a domesticated animal that can provide people with milk as well as dung which can be used as fuel and insulation. The cow gives humans much whilst requiring little in return; what the cow lives on is not used by humans: hay, grass and vegetable waste products.

Killing a cow is regarded as an abomination by Hindus. It is therefore the lowest castes who are required to perform this act when necessary.

SHANGHAI

A couple for whom less is more

BIG CITY BUSTLE, cultural clashes, anach-ronisms. Shanghai is anything other than minimalist. Despite this, or perhaps because of it, simplicity is the keyword for this young Shanghai couple regarding their home and daily lives.

It's early morning in July. The heat, which diminished a little during the night, is beginning to envelope the metropolis of Shanghai.

Qian Chang gets into his car to drive to his office. His wife Yang Yang takes the underground to her job in People's Square. He works in the import and export of chemical dyes. She works in marketing for a French company.

Both have professions that hardly existed twenty years ago.

Both Chang and Yang were born and brought up in the city and are in many ways the model of the new Shanghai; young, successful and trendy. The couple describe themselves as belonging to the upper-middle class and have all of the appropriate attributes: car, dog, annual foreign holidays and an apartment close to the city centre.

Aged thirty, they have seen both the old Shanghai where state coupons were the only currency and today's shiny, futuristic metropolis. Chang and Yang are also examples of a couple who have benefited from the economic wonder that is today's China, with Shanghai at the fore-front.

Yang and Chang met at the beginning of their university studies. They went out together

for eight years before marrying according to Chinese custom and moving in together.

Their apartment is on the sixteenth floor of a high-rise in the Huangpo district of central Shanghai. The windows look out over the Nanpu Bridge, one of the major bridges linking the western part of the city, Puxi, with the eastern part, Pudong. The apartment belonged to Chang's family, but the couple had it completely renovated before moving in. They planned everything themselves and chose everything from floors to bathroom fittings.

They read all of the interior design magazines and tore out pictures of colours, fittings and furniture that they liked. Much of the furniture was specially ordered and made by carpenter according to measurements Chang had taken from designs in the magazines. The living room sofa that the couple found in a Scandinavian design shop was their most expensive purchase, but for Chang the roomy sofa was a necessity:

"I have longer legs than most Chinese men, so normal Chinese-made sofas are simply too small for me. This sofa was designed in Denmark and suits me perfectly," he says, stretching his legs.

Nowadays, many Chinese pay an interior design company to take care of the renovation and decoration of a new home. You only have to say what style you like and the company takes care of the rest: planning, drawing, buying and supervising the work. All you have to do then is move in.

But Chang and Yang looked forward to the actual renovation work. They knew what they wanted and supervised the work themselves.

"I measured everything down to the last centimetre, did the drawings, planned everything, collected business cards from companies that sold paint, furniture, floors or taps that we wanted. Then I gave the drawings and business cards to the workers, who carried out the real hard work."

"Yang came here several times a week to make sure everything was as it should be," Chang explains.

Shanghai has changed a lot in the three years since they moved in. When Chang and Yang moved in together, it was unusual for people under thirty to own their own apartments.

Many young people still live with their parents even after they've married. It's a way of saving money in the increasingly expensive Shanghai. So until very recently, the product range in design shops was aimed at an older, more conservative customer group.

"At that time, not many shops in Shanghai were selling the kind of furniture and fittings that we wanted. We had quite specific requirements so we looked around for several months to find the right furniture, lamps and fittings."

"Our parents' generation collects masses of things so they want as many display surfaces as

BEEF IN HOT BEAN SAUCE

4 portions

500 g sliced back beef or rump steak

1 table spoon + ½ table spoon corn starch

100 ml water

1 table spoon + 1 table spoon Chinese rice wine or dry sherry

1 table spoon +

½ table spoon light soy sauce

2 table spoons vegetable oil

2 tsp finely chopped garlic

2 tsp grated ginger

2 table spoons hot bean sauce

1½ table spoon sugar

1½ tsp white wine vinegar

Place meat in a bowl and sprinkle with 1 table spoon corn starch. Mix well. Add 1 table spoon rice wine and 1 table spoon soy sauce and mix well. Marinate for 10 min.

Mix ½ table spoon corn starch with water.

Heat a wok or large frying pan, pour in oil. Add garlic and ginger when the oil is hot, fry on medium heat for 5 sec.

Increase heat and add the meat. Fry until cooked through, approx. 1–1½ min.

Add bean sauce, 1 table spoon rice wine, ½ table spoon soy sauce, sugar, vinegar and maizena mixture. Stir well. Continue until sauce thickens and clears, approx. 30 sec.

Serve immediately.

WHITE WALLS, WHITE FLOORS,
WHITE SHELVES. A LOT OF
THINGS ARE IN WHITE
TO GIVE THE APARTMENT
A SPACIOUS FEELING.

– if you wanted to get cold drinks in summer, the children were sent with a thermos flask to an ice shop. So when people suddenly had their own money they were naturally very careful with their pennies.

"Our parents bought expensive things – everything had to be in solid wood. Even the ceilings were often covered in wood panelling. They place great importance on the material, it should preferably be mahogany. Their generation regards an apartment as an investment. It has to last for a long time."

"We, on the other hand, can replace things if we get tired of them or feel they don't look good any more," says Chang, and gives an example:

"We might keep a television for a few years and then change it because it's gone out of

龙

possible. For us, the most important thing is that everything should look good and match," explains Yang.

White walls, white floors, white shelves. A lot of things are in white to give the apartment a spacious feeling. Yang and Chang's apartment is 80 m², comparatively large for a Shanghai apartment.

Shanghai is becoming more and more expensive as a place to live, but for the middle class, apartments have grown in parallel with the growth of the city. Until relatively recently, most families lived in a single room. People slept on the sofa and mattresses, which were stored away during the day.

The kitchen was shared with several neighbouring families. There were no refrigerators

fashion. Whereas our parents would watch the same television for ten years or more. We would also like to change our home at regular intervals; you can't live for too long in the same place, there has to be change in our lives." This is perhaps the greatest difference between the generations in today's China.

Yang and Chang have very westernised tastes. With the exception of the large, glamorous wedding photographs that hang above the bed and in the hallway, there is nothing to indicate that the apartment is situated in China's largest city.

But this doesn't mean the couple don't like Chinese furniture design.

"I think Chinese design can be nice, but it doesn't suit us. Firstly, it feels a bit old-fashioned, and secondly, it's very expensive and needs a lot of space in order to look right."

"Our attitude to western style is perhaps the same as foreigners' attitudes to Chinese furniture – that it's exotic and new," Chang remarks.

"But all this white was too much for our parents:"

"They think our home looks like a hospital. They also wonder whether it isn't highly imprac-

tical to have a white floor. But this floor is in laminate and it's easy to keep clean," says Yang.

Early evening, rush-hour traffic, car queues in the evening smog. Chang is sitting in his car on the Yan'an Road, the six lane flyover that goes from east to west through Shanghai. Only cars and skyscrapers are visible through the car windows.

Chang has finished work for the day and is going home via People's Square to pick up Yang. Chang tells us that he finishes work at five, a bit earlier than most people, so that he and Yang normally get home before the rush-hour begins in earnest.

Chang, who has worked at the same company since graduating from university, realises that he is fortunate. His position in the company is stable and he no longer has to work long days in order to prove himself.

"Many people come to this city to earn money. They're prepared to work hard. But I think this applies to cities all over the world. You could choose to live in a smaller town where the pace is slower and you don't have to work as hard, but then there would be fewer opportunities to be successful."

"Nowadays everyone wants to be rich," says Chang.

Yang and Chang usually travel home together, even though Yang could get home on the city's new underground in less than half an hour. Both have a surprisingly positive attitude towards the traffic in a city notorious for its constant traffic chaos.

"The traffic is so much better than it was ten years ago. There was no underground then and I had to spend three or four hours a day on overcrowded buses," says Yang.

Another reason why they make sure that they get home early is Lulu, the couple's white mon-

Today I have everything
I dreamed of – and I
never imagined it would
be so easy to achieve.

grel dog. Lulu is alone all day and is overjoyed when Yang and Chang come home. She seldom gets out – in China it is not unusual to keep dogs indoors all the time.

They obey the calls of nature just like indoor cats in a particular place in the bathroom.

After playing with Lulu, Yang cooks a meal. In the evenings, the couple often stay at home and listen to music or watch films. The piles of DVDs bear witness to many evenings at home on the sofa. Chang and Yang are happiest at home.

But if you live in Shanghai, it's often simpler to eat out than at home. Chinese food in all its forms, Japanese, French, Indian, Italian delicacies, and Mexican fast food; in Shanghai, there's everything.

Restaurants compete with each other in in-ventiveness, both in food and decor. Yang reads the restaurant reviews in the newspaper and ticks off the interesting ones for her and Chang to try out later. They eat out at least two or three times a week.

"If a restaurant is no good we never go back there; in Shanghai there are always new places to visit," Yang tells us.

Weather permitting, they choose places with alfresco service for brunch at the end of the week. The Italian Baci and the Japanese Ambrosia are two of their favourites. The weekend also means a shopping trip to the supermarket in order to fill the refrigerator and buy other essentials.

"We have a very large fridge so we have to buy a lot at a time," laughs Yang.

In China, it is unusual not to have started a

164

family by the age of thirty. But Yang and Chang say they're not in a hurry. A child is probably included in the plans but only in three to five years.

"We'll need a bigger apartment before having a child and there are lots of things to take into consideration: where the child will attend school, what the traffic connections are like, the distance to our parents and so on," says Yang.

"But it won't matter whether it's an apartment block or an old two-story house, as long as it's suitable for us. In Shanghai there are few alternatives because it's so expensive. And it's not a good idea to take out an excessively large mortgage for an expensive apartment. That would be a lifelong burden. Then you wouldn't be able to travel anywhere or do anything at all," says Chang.

This type of thinking reminds us that we are, after all, in China. Economic security is a new phenomenon and is only enjoyed by a privileged few. Stability is the most important thing; having security if something unforeseen happens. Because if it does, you have no one but yourself to rely on.

"That's why we'd rather live slightly below our means rather than above them. Still, in China, lots of people like to show off their wealth. My friends sometimes ask me why we don't have a nicer car or a bigger apartment just because we can afford it, but I don't think that's a good idea. We live well and enjoy our life as it is," says Chang.

One thing that's certain is that neither Yang nor Chang wants to leave Shanghai.

"We were both born and brought up here. We've seen how the city has become better and better and more beautiful. It looks completely different now from when we were children. Everything has changed – the buildings, the infrastructure, the range of products and services. We feel a bit like proud parents: look how well our child has succeeded," says Yang.

Her husband continues:

"When I was younger and studying at university, I thought it would be wonderful to live abroad. But now after having travelled around and seen a few things I no longer think that it's better abroad. I have no desire to leave Shanghai."

"Of course, there are problems here too. The rich-poor gap is growing and it's not good if it gets too big. But at the same time there are fantastic opportunities to get on in Shanghai. Everyone who works hard has the chance of a better life. Our parents' generation didn't have that opportunity," says Chang.

Both seem slightly bemused over how well their lives have worked out. Chang says that his life today exceeds the dreams he had when he was younger:

"When I began studying and imagined my adult life, I thought it would be fantastic to have my own car. But then that was just a distant dream. Today I have everything I dreamed of – and I never imagined it would be so easy to achieve."

– If a restaurant is no good we never go back there; in Shanghai there are always new places to visit, Yang tells us.

SHANGHAI · CHINA

Official name: Zhonghua Renmin Gonghegou/The People's Republic of China

Official language: Chinese

Capital city: Beijing

Area: 9.6 million km²

Population: 1,300 million inhabitants

Population density:
135 inhabitants/km²

Currency: yuan, CNY

Internet users:
632 per 10,000 inhabitants

BAI JIA XING

There aren't many surnames in China; only about 200 of them. Most are collected in the classic *Bai Jia Xing* – The hundred families' surnames.

In China, the surname comes first in a person's name. Women keep their surnames after marriage. Children take their fathers' surnames however.

SHANGHAIED

Shanghai used to be a very attractive place to all seamen who arrived there. Often ships' captains had problems when their ship was due to leave because crew members would be missing.

The seamen would frequent the bar districts and the captains had to go there and literally drag crew members back to their ships. When the seamen woke up, it was too late. The ship was already far out at sea!

This is the origin of the expression "being Shanghaied", meaning to be carried off against your will.

CHINESE FOOD

Chinese cuisine can be roughly divided into four regions: Beijing in northern China, Szechuan in the west, Guangzhou in the south and Shanghai in the east. The climates of the various regions dictate how the food is cooked and which ingredients are used.

The most internationally well-known cuisine is from Guangzhou, since it was from the south of China that most Chinese emigrated.

GANBEI

The word *ganbei* means "dry glass" and it's the expression used when proposing a toast in China. When you have said ganbei and emptied your glass, you hold it upside-down afterwards to show clearly that your glass is empty.

HOROSCOPE

The Chinese use a different kind of horoscope, based on 12 animals: rat, dragon, monkey, ox, snake, cockerel, tiger, horse, dog, rabbit, goat and pig.

If you were born in a certain year, represented by a certain animal, this can be significant to how successful you become and what characteristics you have.

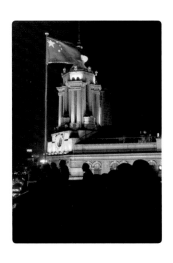

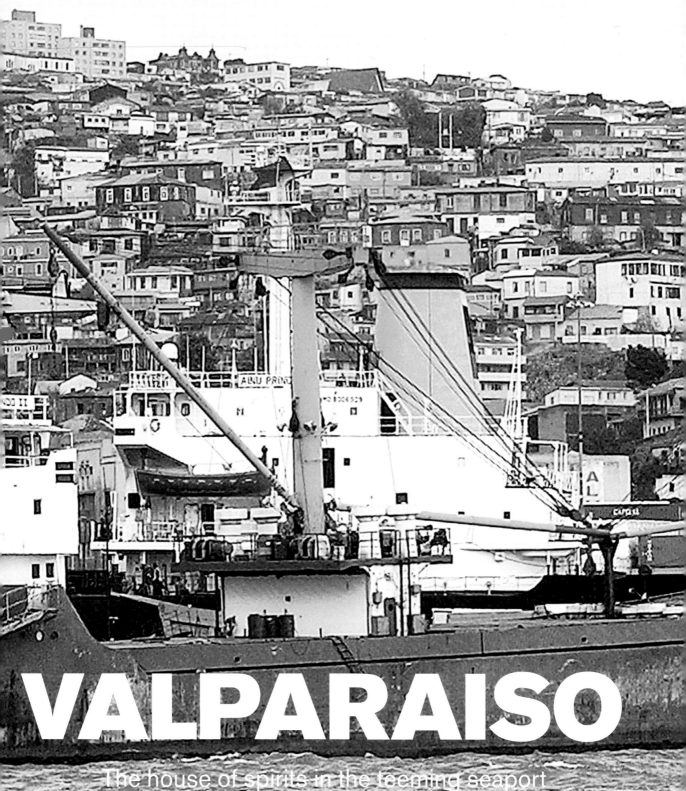

VALPARAISO

The house of spirits in the teeming seaport

THE HOUSE WHERE ARTISTS Salvador Amenábar and Pia Subercaseaux live with their two children, Sara and Ramiro, is much written-about, but almost impossible to find.

The house lies in the centre of town, on Cerro La Loma, one of Valparaiso's 34 hills, not far from Pablo Neruda's house, La Sebastiana, now a busy museum.

Finding the street itself is not difficult. But when you get close to the right number, the street suddenly changes its name in the middle of a bend and all the houses have numbers over 100. The number we're looking for just isn't there.

The explanation, as is usually the case in Valparaiso, is that when the abrupt name change occurs, the street continues alongside in the form of a narrow stone staircase winding between houses which seem to cling to the steep slopes of the hill by sheer willpower.

And there, almost at the bottom, just when the stone stairs take a sudden turn to the left, is a heavy wooden door with the right number barely visible. The door is placed in an ochre coloured wall and appears to lead to an overgrown garden rather than a house.

But something more awaits us.

When the door is opened, it feels as though we've landed in the middle of a story from the Chilean countryside during the last century – like in Isabel Allende's novel *The House of Spirits*.

The house is built around a colourful garden that continues down a staircase. A corridor under a jutting roof runs right round the house. The

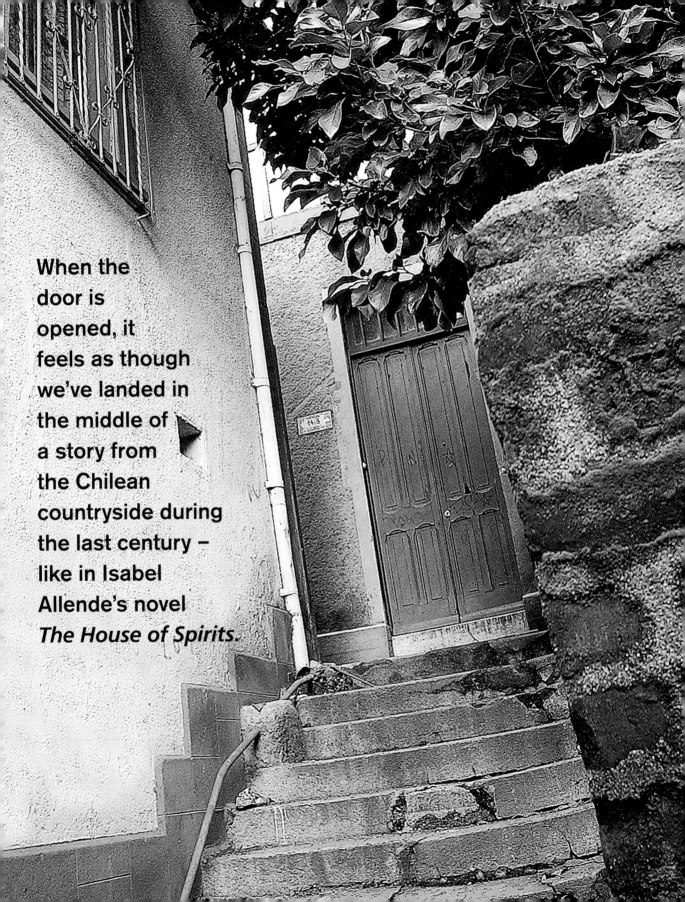

When the door is opened, it feels as though we've landed in the middle of a story from the Chilean countryside during the last century – like in Isabel Allende's novel *The House of Spirits.*

rooms are in a row, like in old houses in the country. On the short, far side of the house, Pia and Salvador have their studio from which there is a view of the sea.

Along the long side are the bedrooms and in the other short side is the kitchen – the obvious heart of the house as Pia says.

There is no living room.

In the kitchen, the rural feeling fades and we return to the urban world which is the real Valparaiso. It feels as though we've finished up in an old seamen's bar down on the docks.

Under the high ceiling hangs a collection of marine signal flags and in one corner is a piano. A long, wide bar which once stood in an inn in Limache divides the kitchen area from the long oak table that Salvador inherited from an aunt and which is the house's natural meeting place even outside mealtimes.

The walls are bright red and on the glass doors out to the garden it says *Standard Bar* in small, straggling letters.

"That was several years ago, long before we moved here. We just happened to be walking by when they were demolishing the Standard Bar, a legendary but very shabby old bar. We succeeded in salvaging the doors, which we stored in an attic for several years until we came here and discovered that they fitted perfectly."

Many of the things in Pia and Salvador's house have similar histories.

"We're incurable collectors," says Salvador.

"At least Salvador is," giggles Pia. "Wherever we go, he finds things to take home with him. They almost always find a place," she adds with a hint of surprise.

"It probably has something to do with the fact that we're incurably nostalgic," she adds. "We long for a way of life that no longer exists."

Both Pia and Salvador's families have roots in *fundos*, the manorial country houses originating from the Spanish colonial power's encomienda system. This was also where Chilean modernity was born.

Pia's grandmother was one of the models for the wise women in *The House of Spirits*. The fundo, Santa Clara, in southern Chile, where her grandmother ruled, is now a ruin. Nonetheless, it's full of traces of the remarkable lives that were lived there, where the latest fashions from Paris mixed easily with the traditions of the Chilean countryside.

Santa Clara had more intensive links with the global metropolises of the time than with Santiago. It was also more deeply rooted in the Chilean soil than the capital.

In many ways, Pia and Salvador's house is a remnant from the Santa Clara period, or rather from the tales of that time with which the couple grew up.

Almost all of their furniture is old. It was found in deserted houses, at jumble sales, but some was also bought.

"But they're not antiques," Salvador quickly points out. "Nothing here is really old. And there's really nothing here of financial value. They're things that tell a story, that breathe, that are full of beauty and craftsmanship, but also, perhaps most importantly, they're functional."

"It might look as if we're collectors in Pablo Neruda's class," says Pia, "but we're not. We want a comfortable home. Comfortable, but beautiful in a way that we like … and maybe also a little magical and mystical, just like Valparaiso."

Both Pia and Salvador are from Santiago and almost all the exhibitions they have held have taken place there. It's there that they have their history and their families.

Why did they come to Valparaiso?

There are many answers to that question. One is that Valparaiso is filled with a magic that exists nowhere else. A major seaport, built on the hills above the cold but proud Pacific Ocean, inhabited by people from all over the world.

A cosmopolitan city, which is modestly provincial at the same time. A city which during the crisis of the 1970s and 80s sank deep into decay, but which has now proudly and happily discovered its rare beauty and has been rewarded for it by UNESCO with a designation as a World Heritage Site.

A city where trolleybuses from the early 1960s are just as numerous as horse carriages but where most cars are of the latest model. A city where old-fashioned shops with counters, half a dozen assistants, shelves up to the ceilings and where you can buy everything, can still compete with modern chain stores.

A town where the lift is an essential means of transport for quickly and safely travelling up the hills.

But Salvador and Pia also have another, simpler explanation:

"We like taking our easels and sitting outside to paint in the middle of reality," says Salvador.

"In Santiago, you're regarded as a clown if you do that. But not here. In Santiago, I would have been forced to live in a studio … closed, shut in. Here, there's both physical and spiritual space, an openness that I would not want to be without."

Both Pia and Salvador are 33 years old. They were born during the emblematic year of 1973, when Augusto Pinochet, General Chief of Staff of the Army, caused the death of the socialist president Salvador Allende in a military coup.

They came to Valparaiso 10 years ago, each in their own way, and it was here that they met.

"But it's changed since then," says Pia.

"In those days, a single woman from Santiago was something of a sensation here. But now this is completely normal. It's almost become a trend."

Many people from Santiago choose to study in Valparaiso these days. A whole artists' colony has emerged, made up of people who have emigrated from Santiago. And younger professional people have begun buying summer houses here instead of in the bathing resorts to the north and south of Valparaiso.

After several years in a sort of depressive coma, Valparaiso has woken up and been discovered, not only by other Chileans, but by tourists from all over the world.

In parallel with Chile's economic growth, the port has gained new life and, along with it, the whole town.

Old houses on the hills that appeared derelict have begun to be restored. House walls that hadn't been painted or maintained for decades have been given new colours. Dark, cobbled streets have been given street lighting. Inns and bars with exciting international menus and sophisticated decor have given life to what were formerly dead old buildings. It's simmering and bubbling with life and Valparaiso is no longer a mystical town only in old sailors' stories.

And additionally, the port is at last on its way to becoming part of the town and not, as it has been before, a wall between town and sea.

When Pia and Salvador first saw the house, they decided at once that they definitely did not want to live there.

"The house had been empty for two years. The owner, a widow, had been taken into an old people's home and the only inhabitant was

They're things
that tell a story,
that breathe,
that are full of beauty
and craftsmanship,
but also, and perhaps
most importantly,
they're functional.

a dog that survived only because neighbours threw food over the wall to it."

"It was extremely dirty and overgrown with wild plants. There was nothing inviting about it at all. The neighbours also said that it was haunted."

"But," says Salvador, "several months later I suddenly woke up at about five in the morning and sat up in bed. I'd had a sort of revelation and I shook Pia's shoulder until she woke up. 'Pia,' I said, 'that's the house that we should buy …' There's no doubt about it; that's the house."

"The same day, I set the wheels in motion for buying the house." That was four years ago. Now everything's different.

But despite the dilapidation, they haven't changed much in the house. Glass roofs in the bedrooms to let in more light; a few repairs; but most of all, clearing out and cleaning.

The house is built of adobe – thick, sturdy walls that keep the heat in when it's cold and stay cool in when the summer heat arrives.

One of the most important tasks was to paint the walls both inside and outside.

"We discovered the colours in the different types of earth around the town and we used earth as a raw material to create the colours we wanted," Pia tells us. "But it took time before we made it what it is now."

"The kitchen was blue at first, then green and now it's red. Each room grows with its own colour … and each room has changed its form many times."

"But," says Pia, "we've done most work on the garden.

Here there are flowers and fruit trees from all over Chile. Plants that we've taken with us during our journeys around the country:

CEVICHE

4 persons

350 g firm, filleted fish (if you use salmon it must have been frozen first)

1 white onion

1 red or green chilli

2 table spoons fresh coriander

3 lemons

salt, pepper

1 avocado

½ peeled cucumber

1 tomato

lettuce leaves

Finely chop the onion, chilli, coriander and fish. Mix the ingredients in a glass bowl.

Squeeze lemon over mixture so that fish is well covered. Cover with plastic and place in refrigerator, allow to marinate for at least 6 hours. When fish is ready it will be white and firm in consistency.

Season with salt and pepper.

Serve the fish as it is in small bowls, or mix with chopped avocado, tomato, cucumber and lettuce.

You can also serve the ceviche with fruits such as mango and melon. Their sweetness goes well with the heat and acidity.

WE'VE DONE
MOST WORK ON
THE GARDEN

camomille, chirimoya, oranges, lemons and even bananas, that have grown and this year will be giving us their first harvest, despite the fact that the climate in Valparaiso is far from tropical. It's hardly even Mediterranean."

There are some small goldfish ponds. Salvador says that he would like to build ponds everywhere, but he's so preoccupied with his painting that he doesn't have time. In the beginning, they had some doves and a few pheasants, but Salvador opened the cage doors so that they could move about more freely. And that's exactly what they did. They never came back.

"And that was probably the right thing," says Salvador laconically.

"Actually," says Pia as we're drinking a glass of wine from a store that Salvador has in a cellar under the kitchen table, "this is not a particularly beautiful house. There are lots of other houses in Valparaiso that are more beautiful, with glass verandas and clear views over the sea, with large rooms and a design that allows for a more private life than here, where nobody can shut themselves away because all the rooms are linked."

"But," she says, "this was the house that chose us, and this is our world."

"Perhaps," she says, "we can say without being arrogant, that our house is also a picture; the most beautiful that any of us has yet painted."

VALPARAISO · CHILE

Official name: República de Chile/ Republic of Chile

Official language: Spanish

Capital city: Santiago

Area: 757,000 km²

Population: 16 million inhabitants

Population density: 21 inhabitants/km²

Currency: Chilean peso, CLP

Internet users: 2,720 per 10,000 inhabitants

COLOURFUL

The house facades of Valparaiso are extremely colourful and it is said that this is a recent phenomenon. The town's mayor offered all house owners free paint if they paid unemployed people to do the work. In this way, the mayor killed two birds with one stone, the town was made more beautiful and jobs were created.

THE FLAG

According to a modern interpretation, the Chilean flag's colours; white, blue and red symbolise the snow of the Andes, the sky and the people's fight for freedom. The white star stands for the future.

THE WORLD'S LONGEST COUNTRY

Chile is 4,300 km long and is the world's longest and narrowest country. Thanks to its length, the country has several different climates and types of weather; from dry deserts in the north to large ice sheets and glaciers in the south.

The central regions of the country are dominated by a Mediterranean climate, which is good for agriculture and viticulture.

EASTER ISLAND

Easter Island lies in the middle of the Pacific Ocean and belongs to Chile

despite the fact that it is situated 3,780 km west of the country. It's a small triangular island with around 2,000 inhabitants. The Island is famous because it is furthest from all the world's continents. But perhaps above all for its famous stone statues, said to represent the forefathers of the indigenous population, the Long Ears.

The indigenous population claims to have come from Polynesia and not from South America. This is supported by the fact that the statues are reminiscent of Tahiti's Tiki figures.

THE ENCOMIENDA SYSTEM

The encomienda system was very important when the Spanish colonised South America. The Spanish word *encomienda* means to entrust.

The system was based on a group of Indians being entrusted to a colonist by representatives of the government. This representative was meant to protect and convert the Indians to Christianity, who in turn would pay taxes to him.

SYDNEY

Vitality and verve – the Bitton family

WHEN THE BITTON FAMILY were considering their second house purchase, they couldn't resist the colourful suburb of Erskineville. Its position on the southern edge of town, with city centre, harbour and beach all within reach, fitted the family's lifestyle perfectly.

Erskineville is one of the most desirable and family-friendly suburbs of Sydney. This is because of the range of cafés, restaurants and pubs, and in no small measure, its many parks and gardens.

In recent years, Erskineville has developed from grunge to inner-city chic. Characterised by an industrial past and a working class in blue overalls, the suburb offers a pulsating multiculturalism. Since young investors began fighting over the properties in the early 1980s, Erskineville has become an enclave for all types of people with a taste for fashionable living.

Conveniently for David, 37, his wife Sohani, 34, and their three year-old daughter Monet, their work, childcare, relatives and friends lie within easy reach of their home.

David runs a picturesque café in the neighbouring suburb of Alexandria and an upmarket restaurant and wine bar in Kings Cross. At the same time, he produces a series of jams, jellies, oils, marinades and tapanades for his own food brand. Now and then he is also landlord in nearby Redfern. Sohani used to help out in the café, but now works as a business developer for a travel agent.

Like many of today's Australians, David is an immigrant. At the age of 22, he decided to leave the future that had been mapped out for him in France and try a life in Australia instead. He'd only heard about the country from some Australians that he met in Switzerland where he worked at the time. When he came to Sydney in 1991, all he had with him was a suitcase, a little money and the invaluable experience of an apprenticeship in a Paris restaurant.

Within six months he'd met Sohani. She was a waitress and in the process of finishing off her hotel training.

"It was love at first sight," admits David. "I was the young French chef with an arrogant attitude and she hated me."

A lot of hard work and many meetings later they realised they were soul mates.

Australia's cultural melting pot, plus the country's relaxed attitude to food, motivated David to open the doors to his café in 2000. The French/modern Australian café gets a little extra character from the personnel, who come from six different countries. The interior design is a sensitive balance of French and international influences.

The home is the epicentre of the dynamic Bitton family's universe. A typical day for Sohani begins at six o'clock. Once she's prepared herself, she gets Monet ready for the crèche. David, who has been at work since five, drives home to fetch them both, just in time for a family breakfast at the café. If the queue is not too long, David can sit for a while at the breakfast table. After break-

fast, Sohani leaves Monet at the crèche and goes off to work.

After closing the café at around four in the afternoon, David fetches Monet at the crèche and spends some quality time with her in the nearby park.

"This is our time together and we speak only French with each other."

The park is just across the street from the café and only a short walk from the crèche.

Before it's time for David to go off to the restaurant, he and Monet fetch Sohani from work and they spend some time together in the car.

While David is working, Sohani and Monet are at home getting ready for the next day.

David values all the time he can spend with his family; he admits he hasn't spent much time at home since starting the restaurant at the beginning of the year. The couple agree that it's a big undertaking.

"It was a step that had to be taken. The company is an important part of our lives but we have set up a goal for our business and don't plan to carry on like this for the rest of our lives."

The restaurant provides a subdued environment in the midst of the lively and slightly crazy King's Cross. The decor is reminiscent of the Mediterranean and Middle East. Their intention is to create a new trend in dining: the art of sharing.

There are no set starters, main courses or desserts, just lots of small dishes intended for sharing. This creates the environment in which

European dishes and wines have been reintroduced to the menu at affordable prices.

"People have the misconception that European wines are too expensive, but it doesn't need to be like that," explains David.

On the few days that the whole Bitton family has off, they make sure they can enjoy the pleasures of city life together.

On Sundays, they visit Sohani's parents. Because David has no relatives in Australia, he has close contact with his parents-in-law.

"I trust their judgement completely." So no business decisions are taken without his mother-in-law.

"She's got what it takes when it really counts," considers David.

At home, David and Sohani's different backgrounds have made their mark on the interior. Sohani, who was born in South Africa, is of Indian origin. The union between her own and David's cultural inheritances creates an exciting mix. The interior is minimalist, with just enough design details to fill the spaces without feeling crowded.

In the hundred year old two-storey terraced house, Sohani alone is responsible for the interior design.

"I don't think you can learn taste from anyone else. You've either got it or you haven't. I think she's got it," says David.

Sohani explains that her Indian roots have given her a weakness for rich, lively colours.

"Maybe people with different cultural backgrounds don't experience colours in the same way as I do."

Sohani's favourite room is the bedroom with the fuchsia-coloured back wall. Three dark lilac, green and golden paintings over the bedhead, flanked by two green bedside lamps, create balance and warmth in the room together with the floor and bedside tables.

Comfort, warmth and simplicity characterise the home; a place where you can sit back and relax after a busy day. Candles and Buddhas have been placed in almost all of the rooms. The candles create calm and the Buddhas are a symbol of Sohani's spiritual heritage.

"They're a link with my cultural inheritance and give a spiritual dimension to our home environment," she explains.

David and Sohani have chosen to buy their furniture in small furniture shops. They keep their eyes open for these shops when they're out travelling.

"Last time we travelled to Hunter Valley, we stumbled upon a little French/Indian furniture shop. It was unbelievable to find a shop with that particular mixture. It suited our style so perfectly that we bought almost everything they had."

After the birth of their daughter, the way they use their rooms changed: the main entrance leads onto the television room, which Monet occupies.

Monet's other play-space is her bedroom with its own balcony. There she has her stereo, her paintings and lots of books.

"We've made Monet's room into a place where she can relax, read, play and feel comfortable," says David.

Most energy has been invested in the dining room and the sophisticated kitchen, David's own domain.

"This is my world, my other baby."

It was totally renovated when they moved in. It's chef-friendly and fitted out entirely in stainless steel, in accordance with David's strict requirement.

David's pride and joy is his wine cellar. Amongst other things, it's home to his collection of Australian Grange Hermitage which he began in 1991.

"So when my daughter reaches 21, I'll have a good 21st birthday present for her and she can then carry on the tradition to the next generation."

Like most houses in inner-city Sydney, this one has very limited outdoor space, but there's room for a luxurious outdoor grill and some wooden outdoor furniture. Even though Sohani would rather have had a large garden, she understands that this is the price you pay for living so centrally.

"The suburban brick houses simply don't feel as genuine as those in the inner city."

It's also about location: being able to walk instead of taking the car.

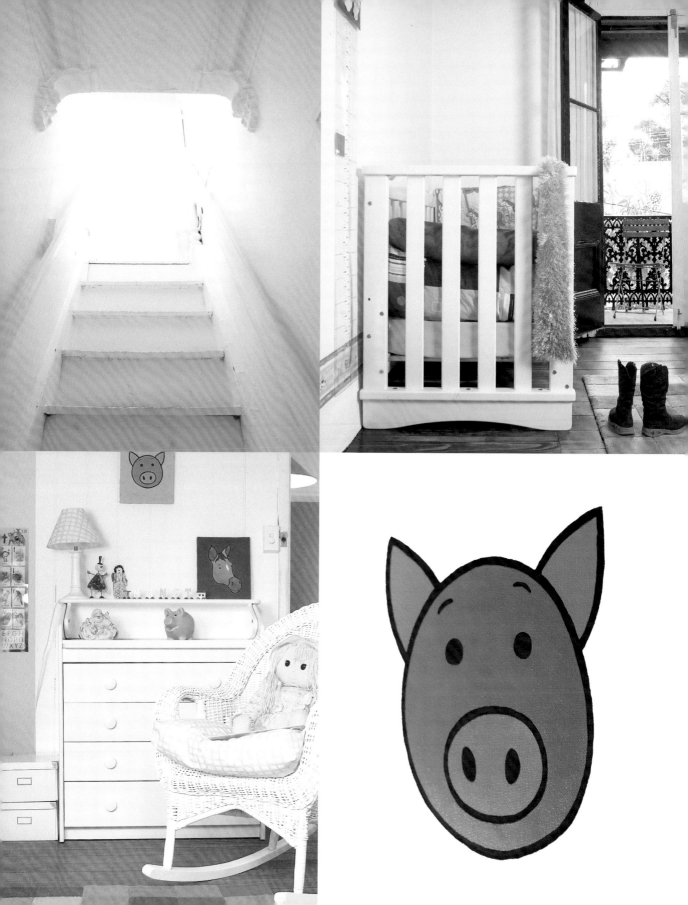

"I love just being able to put Monet in the pushchair and take a walk to our café or to my sister or friends who live in the area," says Sohani.

The surrounding parks and gardens also offer a change in environment for the Bitton family.

Sydney can offer a dynamic lifestyle. A lifestyle which, with the aid of hard work, can be achieved more easily here than in the places that David and Sohani come from.

"Here you work for your lifestyle, not just to survive," says Sohani.

"The people are the special thing about Sydney," adds David and continues:

"The interplay that comes from the meeting of different cultures."

Allowing Monet to experience cultural diversity is an important part of her upbringing, according to David and Sohani. Australians are generally good at enjoying life and not taking themselves too seriously.

The hardworking couple plan to place Monet in an international school in the future. Eventually, David hopes to rest on his laurels and slow down the pace of his work. Sohani confesses that she would have nothing against retiring in the south of France. But at the moment, and like thousands of others in Sydney, the family is content to enjoy city life and everything about it.

Skewered tiger prawns with honey and lime butter *6 portions*

200 g unsalted butter at room temperature
6 cl dry, white wine
8 cl freshly squeezed lime juice
1½ tbsp mild honey
2½ cm peeled and grated ginger

1 tbsp finely chopped garlic
paprika powder
24 peeled giant prawns
6 sprigs of fresh coriander
3 limes in segments

Place 12 skewers in water for around 20 minutes. Heat oven grill to max. temperature.

Mix the butter, wine, lime juice, honey, ginger and garlic into a smooth paste. Season with powdered paprika. Spoon the mixture into a thick-bottomed saucepan and melt over low heat, simmer for 5 min. to allow tastes to mix properly.

Cover a plate or large tin with oven foil. Allow skewers to drip-dry, then thread the giant prawns onto each skewer. Place skewers on oven plate and brush prawns with the aromatic butter.

Grill prawns in oven, turning at least once and brush generously with butter. After approx. 2 min. on each side, the prawns should be ready.

Remove prawns from skewers and serve them with sliced lime.

SYDNEY · AUSTRALIA

Official name:
Commonwealth of Australia

Official language: English

Capital city: Canberra

Area: 7.7 million km²

Population: 20.1 million inhabitants

Population density:
3 inhabitants/km²

Currency: Australian dollar, AUD

Internet users:
5,667 per 10,000 inhabitants

CAPITAL

Australia's capital is Canberra. In the aborigines' language, this means "meeting place".

Canberra is situated between the major cities of Sydney and Melbourne. When a decision was being made as to the location of Australia's capital, no one could agree on whether Sydney or Melbourne should have this honour. So they simply built a city between them, and Canberra was born.

DANGEROUS ANIMALS

Six of the world's ten most dangerous snakes live in Australia. Two of them are included in the list of Australia's most dangerous animals:

❶ Box jellyfish *Cubomedusae*

❷ Irukandji jellyfish *Carukia barnesi*

❸ Salt water crocodile/Delta crocodile *Crocodylus porosus*

❹ Blue-ringed jellyfish *Hapalochlaena*

❺ Stonefish *Synanceiidae*

❻ Redback spider *Latrodectus hasselti*

❼ Brown snake *Pseudonaja textilis*

❽ Tiger snake *Notechis scutatus*

❾ White shark *Carcharodon carcharias*

❿ Funnel-web spider *Atrax robustus*

SMALL CONTINENT

Australia with the rest of Oceania is the world's smallest continent and the world's largest inhabited island.

SYDNEY OPERA HOUSE

The Sydney Opera House was designed in 1957 by the Danish architect Jørn Utzon. It was inaugurated sixteen years later by the British Queen. The Opera House has a very special design and is built from 1,056,000 bricks which were made in Höganäs in Sweden.

GRANNY SMITH

The crisp, green Granny Smith apple was originally developed by Maria Smith in Eastwood, New South Wales in the 1860s.

REYKJAVÍK

Light and warmth in the angels' house

THE HOUSE WE ARE GOING TO VISIT is no ordinary house. On first inspection, it looks like a transformer station: tall, square and cement grey. Really quite dull.

If you stop at the house, look again and give yourself a little time, you'll soon discover that it's a lovely house, a house with intrinsic beauty.

No, this is no ordinary house like all the others standing on the street battling with wind and rain (the normal weather in Reykjavík and the rest of Iceland). Hardly a summer day passes without a heavy rain shower and in winter, there's rain and snow to struggle through on the way to work, school or whatever other business you might be engaged in.

The house was designed by the architect Brynjar Brynjarsson and built in 1942 whilst the Second World War raged. It was commissioned by the famous Icelandic artist Jón Engilberts as a place to live and work. Originally intended to be even bigger with extensions in geometrical forms of various sizes, the plans were never realised because there was never really enough money. Today, four angels live in the house. On the facade of the house, the name Englaborg (Castle of the Angels) is moulded into the plaster, rather like a packaging label. Its inhabitants are Sigtryggur Bjarni Baldvinsson, 40, and Tinna Gunnarsdóttir, 38 with their two children. They are Hallbjörg Embla, who is eight years old and enjoys drawing, pottering about and playing games, and Tryggvi Kolvidur, who is six and the best footballer in the world.

He's an artist. She's a designer.

"Velkommina inn," says Tinna when we ring the doorbell. "Please excuse the mess. But with children in the house it looks just as messy 15 minutes later, even if you've just cleaned up."

If the house appears a little sombre and bunker-like from the outside, you're immediately struck by how light it is when you get inside.

As soon as you get into the hall it's light, warm and inviting. And in the other rooms the light continues to stream in.

"When I was little, I often used to pass this house on the way to and from my ballet lessons. Even then, I knew there was something different about it. I asked my mother and she told me about the artist and his family who lived here," Tinna tells us.

Later, when she grew older, she forgot about the house. Until nine years ago. Tinna and Sigtryggur had won artists' scholarships and at that time were living in a tiny flat in Milan. Their first child was on its way and it was time to return home to Reykjavík.

"That summer, we met my parents in London and my father told me that the house was for sale and that he thought we should buy it. So we did, without even having seen it properly inside, apart from in pictures," continues Tinna.

"It was probably the best thing we'll ever do in our lives. Prices were low and no one wanted to live in old houses. At that time it had to be modern, newly built and a bit flashy. But also because it's an absolutely outstanding house with a lot of soul and atmosphere."

"THE HEART OF THE HOUSE," SAYS SIGTRYGGUR WITHOUT ANY HESITATION. "WE SPEND MOST OF OUR TIME HERE."

For their first year in the house, Sigtryggur and Tinna didn't know what to do with it.

"The house was in need of considerable renovation, but we were worried its character would be lost if we started that. You see, there had been an idea behind the house when it was built and we wanted it to live on."

"Come with me and I'll show you round," says Tinna. We take our shoes off, because that's what people do in Iceland where it's almost always wet outside and you don't want to bring the dirt in with you.

We view the house in our socks. After the hall we come into the living room. It's light, airy and has lots of pictures on the walls. Some were painted by Sigtryggur, others by artist friends.

Inside the living room, behind a screening wall with a passage on each side, is the kitchen and eating area.

"The heart of the house," says Sigtryggur, without any hesitation. "We spend most of our time here."

Not just at dinner time, but also when the children are doing their homework and when friends and neighbours drop in for a cup of coffee. And also when darkness falls over Reykjavík and it's time to end the day with a chat before bedtime.

On the floor above is Sigtryggur's artist's studio, designed by the house's first artist Jón Engilberts. It's a beautiful, symmetrical room with a big panoramic window on the short side of the house, a window that begins just over a metre from the floor and goes on all the way up to the ceiling.

The light filters in gently and since it faces north it leaves no shadows. This is a rather important detail for someone who is painting and dependent on controlling light and shadows so they don't play unwanted tricks.

Sigtryggur spends his days here with tubes of paint, brushes and turpentine. Paintings are born here depicting the constant changes and cycles of nature.

In the studio it's quiet, with an almost sacred peace.

"That's how I want it," says Sigtryggur. Concentration requires silence. Reflection also requires silence.

In the room next door, Tinna has her workplace. Here she conceives her ideas for various products: stools, chairs, tables and many other things. These will be manufactured and launched in Iceland and elsewhere in the world.

Another project involves various large spheres of lava being placed out in the garden as sculptures. The surface is even and smooth but at the same time perforated with tiny hollows. Time will show which plants or mosses will put down roots.

This is the house. Two floors, four rooms, a small practical kitchen, a hall and a guests' toilet. But where do people sleep?

"In the cellar of course," says Tinna.

On the floor below, the family have installed their bedrooms. The children each have a favourite colour. And the parents' bedroom has an exit and staircase out to the garden.

Here too, the light streams in, despite the fact that it's under the ground. The windows, at ceiling height along the whole long side of the house, let in large amounts of daylight. This is reflected in the light, harmonious colours of the walls.

Here in the cellar there is also a large tiled bathroom, a storeroom and a combined laundry and carpenter's workshop. It could be tidier, as Tinna points out when we look in.

A little detail, which might raise the odd eyebrow, is that there's no boiler, despite the cold, grim Icelandic climate. The explanation is simple. The house isn't heated by electricity; heat comes instead from the volcanic hot water which is so abundant on Iceland and which provides almost all households with cheap heating.

Back in the kitchen, Sigtryggur prepares for the evening meal. He usually takes charge of the cooking. Today it's going to be cod, typical Icelandic fare that has been eaten for generations.

"We Icelanders are very lucky in this respect. We have fantastic native food products. Fresh fish of every kind; and fantastic lamb too which is ... how should I describe this ... marinated from

the inside because the barren earth from which the animals graze is covered in grass with a certain saltiness from the sea and the wild herbs," he explains to us.

"Perhaps this is why there are so many fantastically good restaurants on Iceland. You can eat really well almost anywhere, and Reykjavík is probably the capital city in the world with the most gourmet restaurants per head of population."

Tinna, who is seated at the kitchen table, agrees:

"It only takes five minutes to get to the centre of Reykjavík. We used to go out quite a lot, but now the children take up more and more time and we prioritise things that we can do together as a family."

Instead of late nights at the restaurant, the family often take day trips out to the country.

"We like to pack a tent, sleeping bags and primus stove and just drive straight out into the wilderness."

"In some places nature is extra generous. There are places here and there where you can bathe in warm springs. The temperature's just right, so you don't get scalded," Tinna tells us.

Another popular treat for the whole family, especially in winter, is to visit one of the many outdoor pools in Reykjavík and swim in water heated by the underground springs.

"Just imagine lying on your back in the beautiful water and looking up at a crystal-clear, starry sky, or swimming around in a heavy snow-storm without feeling the slightest bit cold," says Tina.

Even though the house was once the home of one

of Iceland's most famous artists, it's not a museum. Though the artist's widow would have liked to convert it into one after her husband died.

"No, it's not like that. And it must never become one. We want to preserve the soul of the house. But above all it should be a house that's lived in," says Sigtryggur.

"When we decorated the house, we did it according to our own tastes. We've chosen light walls and linoleum floor coverings in order to make it a little warmer and cosier. We want the art that's hanging on the walls to be seen and to tell its story."

"And our furniture is mostly things that we've found on the street that have been thrown into containers and which we've then rescued. I don't like just buying things and then throwing them away. I would rather preserve old things, and by that I don't mean antiques but perhaps things from the 1950s and 60s," Tinna continues.

"The sofa in the living room is a typical example. We found it on the street one morning. We brought it home and did it up again. All it needed was new fabric and it was as good as new again."

It's the same with the things on the window sills in the house. A lot of it came from flea markets and second-hand shops in Reykjavík. Other things are the kitschy souvenirs from foreign holidays, business trips and the like. The stones, seashells and bits of wood are treasures we found on long walks by the sea."

But perhaps the most important piece of furniture in the house is the old secretaire in the kitchen near the table.

... STONES,
SEASHELLS AND
BITS OF WOOD
ARE TREASURES
WE FOUND ON
LONG WALKS
BY THE SEA.

"It comes from my great grandfather who lived in an isolated little farmhouse out in the country. It brings back memories from when I was a little girl and visited there. I can still smell the smells and hear the voices when I look at it. It means a great deal to me despite the fact that it's not particularly old and many people would certainly think it's pretty ugly."

And so we walk out into the garden. Its' dazzling by Icelandic standards. Cultivating flowers and vegetables here requires green fingers and lots of patience.

"It's the climate," says Sigtryggur shaking his head. "If we have a heatwave, it's 17–20 degrees for a day or two, but normally it stays between 10 and 15 in the summer."

But Tinna and Sigtryggur's garden can still boast rose bushes and a vegetable plot.

"It's all about finding hardy varieties that can cope with our extreme conditions. But if it's hard to get things to grow, you get even more satisfaction when you succeed. I'm extremely proud of my salad plantation, and the strawberry plants that don't ripen until the end of August or the beginning of September. If the weather's been good, that is," he continues, brandishing a bunch of Korean salad.

Out in the garden, the eye is once again drawn to the grey house which is finished with a mixture of cement and lava. Here and there, you can see niches, one large and several small ones on both the long and the short sides.

"Jón Engilberts, the artist who built the house, planned to decorate it with his own paintings. But it never happened. We've been wondering whether we should make his idea a reality. But it's a big project and it will have to be good. It'll have to be something that both we and passers-by will be able to put up with for many years. And we don't want to annoy people."

But a house that's already beautiful, despite its sparse exterior at first glance, would certainly be even more beautiful with murals. And a bit less like a transformer station at first sight for anyone hurrying past on the street who doesn't take the time to stop and look properly.

GARDAR'S LAVA BREAD

250 g crushed rye	1 dessert spoon bicarbonate
250 g crushed wheat	1 l soured milk
150 g linseed	250 ml dark syrup
200 ml raisins	butter
40 g wheat bran	optional breadcrumbs
500 g wheat flour	

Heat the oven to 150 °C.

Mix all the ingredients. The dough must not ferment.

Grease two 1½ litre forms. Pour the mixture into the forms and bake on the lowest shelf for 90 minutes.

In Iceland, this bread is baked in hot lava.
It takes 24 hours. But here we use normal oven heat.
Halve the quantities for just one loaf, and use a shorter baking time (70 minutes).

REYKJAVÍK · ICELAND

Official name: Lýðhveldið Ísland/
The Republic of Iceland

Official language: Icelandic

Capital city: Reykjavik

Area: 103,000 km²

Population: 290,570 inhabitants

Population density:
3 inhabitants/km²

Currency: Icelandic kronor, ISK

Internet users:
6,747 per 10,000 inhabitants

BAY OF SMOKE

Reykjavik is named after the pillars of steam from the hot springs. The word literally means "bay of smoke".

NATURAL ENERGY

The hot springs situated around Reykjavik heat around 55% of the homes in the area. The houses that are not heated by the springs use oil or electricity.

Hot water from the springs also heats the outdoor swimming pools which can be used all year round.

Iceland is the only country in Europe that uses renewable natural resources.

TELEPHONE DIRECTORY

Icelandic telephone directories use a special system. They're arranged alphabetically, but according to the initial of the subscriber's first name instead of surname. This is done

because a person's first name is the important, official name in Iceland. It's your first name that you hand on to your children. Your surname reveals who your father is, for example Kristín Einarsdóttir is the daughter of Einar and Páll Einarsson is the son of Einar.

THE ICELANDIC PONY

The special thing about the Icelandic Pony is its special gait, known as a "tölt". The tölt can be described as a kind of trotting style which is very comfortable for a rider because he or she is not shaken up and down in the saddle.

The pony was brought to Iceland by pioneers around 800 A.D. and the breed has remained the same due to Iceland's isolated geography. It has now become a natural part of the landscape and in the countryside the ponies can graze freely in large herds.

DISCOVERY OF AMERICA

It was not the Italian Christopher Columbus who first set foot on American soil, but an Icelander, Leifr Eriksson, who arrived there 500 years earlier.

After Iceland was colonised, some Icelanders sailed westward towards Greenland. One man, Bjarni Herjólfsson, wandered even farther west and told Leifr that he had seen land, but that he had no desire to sail there. Leifr did however, and he put together a crew and sailed there to see if it was true. So he became the first European to set foot in North America. He called the place Vinland.

His discovery was recorded through the oral tradition until it was written down in the sagas of Vinland and Greenland.